# A GAY CENTURY

PETER SUTT -
IRELAND

homopromos@gmail.
com
07444 311695

*A Gay Century*

Published by The Conrad Press in the United Kingdom 2021

Tel: +44(0)1227 472 874
www.theconradpress.com
info@theconradpress.com

ISBN 978-1-913567-83-5

Printed and bound in Great Britain by Clays Ltd, Elcograf S.p.A

Typesetting and Cover Design by The Book Typesetters,
www.thebooktypesetters.com

This book has been typeset in Adobe Garamond Pro, Gill Sans MT and Salted Monthoers

Illustrations by David Shenton

The Conrad Press logo was designed by Maria Priestley.

# A Gay Century

## Volume One: 1900–1962

*10 unreliable vignettes of Lesbian and Gay Life*

## Peter Scott-Presland

# CONTENTS

*To Robert Ely, who has set these libretti*
*to music so brilliantly.*

# INTRODUCTION

No false modesty. These libretti are the basis for the most ambitious, the most enormous, the most wide-ranging pieces of gay music theatre ever devised. I wanted to publish them, having performed them as rehearsed Zoom readings during lockdown: from the reaction of the audiences I realised that they also stood as little plays in their own right.

*A Gay Century* is a cycle of gay chamber operas covering the period 1900 (death of Oscar Wilde) to 2001 (first civil partnerships introduced in London experimentally by Mayor Ken Livingstone). I originally intended that there would be one for each decade, but it has grown in the writing, so there are now seventeen, making the completed work longer than the *Ring Cycle*. This volume contains the first ten libretti, the rest will be in Volume Two.

It has grow'd like Topsy. Originally, my friend Andrew Lumsden told me a story about an older friend of *his*, who was around eighty years old at the turn of the millennium. And that friend told Andrew the story of how as a teenager he had met Oscar Wilde's lover, Bosie, Lord Alfred Douglas. It was a sweet, sad, story, full of regret, and my reaction was that it would make a superb one-act opera, a kind of reversal of Benjamin Britten's *Death in Venice*, told from the point of view of Tadzio. This became *1935/6: Fishing*.

Having written that, it seemed a bit slight for a full evening's entertainment, so it needed another one-act piece to complement it. What better subject that Wilde's other lover, his first love Robert Ross? Ross had been something of a hero of mine, for his honesty, his loyalty, and his exemplary courage. Reading around the subject, I came across a diary of Siegfried Sassoon which contains an entry for the end of World War One, when a quiet farewell evening with Ross – they had been lovers too – was interrupted by a bumptious young actor and his friend. The young actor was Noël Coward. Here was the germ of a sequence: the idea that people influence each other, for good or ill, down the generations; that there is a torch of a kind to be handed down. Now I had *1918: Front*.

Having got that, it seemed only natural to go back to the iconic figure behind Douglas and Ross, Oscar Wilde himself, as a starting point. Not that Wilde himself was in any sense a founding father – others came before – but he died as the twentieth century began, and the century seemed a meaningful time frame. The antithesis of Wilde was Queen Victoria, the epitome of 'Victorian values', the embodiment of repression who signed into law the Labouchère amendment under which Wilde was imprisoned. I had always harboured the secret thought that Lady Bracknell was Wilde's comic portrait of Victoria. They had to meet, and meet they did, in *1900: Two Queens*. This acts as the prologue to the whole cycle, and gives it its dialectical backbone: the eternal struggle between repression and liberation. I was gratified later to see Rupert Everett's excellent biographical film, *The Happy Prince*, featured a brief encounter between the two.

One a decade… Ideas come and go, but it was important to find a story – not an idea or theme or subject, but a concrete story – which had the shape of a 45–60 minute opera, which could be done with minimal resources, and specifically no more than seven performers.

I had an old composer friend, Robert Ely, with whom I'd worked on a project with the London Gay Symphony Orchestra, an anti-Requiem called *Free*. He was one of seven composers on that project, and one whom I had in my mind as someone I wanted to work with again.

Robert was an acclaimed military band leader and award-winning arranger in a number of regimental bands, ending as Senior Bandmaster of the Parachute Regiment. He was cashiered from the Army in 1986, when they discovered he was gay, and went on to campaign for the rights of LGBT service personnel. He is hugely prolific, a prize-winner, and should have far more recognition than he currently has. He is also a joy to work with.

We agreed from the start that each opera would be a one-act piece, and would involve no more than seven performers in total – 3 actors, 4 musicians or 4 actors and 3 musicians, for example. They were to be aimed at the numerous pop-up opera companies in the UK and US – companies with limited resources, but a commitment to new and exciting work and to taking opera out of the opera house to the people.

This added to the limitations we had to work with. As a result there are probably many strands of the story of gay life and liberation over the period of a hundred years which have been left out. Most obviously it is *A Gay Century*, not an LGBT [or, save the mark! an LGBTQIA+] century. It is written from the perspective of two white gay men about the English experience.

That being said, I wanted to avoid a straightforward rehash of well-known stories, or standard flag-wavers. It is not a didactic cycle, I hope, though the sense of a gradual development of an identity, a consciousness and a sense of self-worth should emerge through the individual characters and stories.

One question I have often been asked is, 'Are these stories true?' Some are, some aren't, and some are half-true. I didn't want to have just a parade of famous names, but the danger of writing about 'ordinary' gays in the past is that we impose a modern sensibility on them; they become Us in funny clothes out of the Lucy Worsley dressing-up box. As a result of this, the rich and famous tend to take a back seat in *A Gay Century* the closer we get to the present [or *my* present, which starts somewhere towards the end of the 1950s]. The truth or otherwise is discussed in the introductions to the individual projects.

As I write this, Robert has finished the music to some twelve of the seventeen operas, which is no mean feat in two and a half years. Whether they make it to the operatic stage in full productions will be a matter of luck, persistence and the good sense of producers. In their pocket opera format they seem made for these straitened coronaviral times.

I have included notes as to the instrumentation used in the score, and the range of the singer for each part. I hope this will help the reader to *hear* each character – and perhaps encourage a producer and/or a pop-up opera company to take a punt on one or more of the pieces.

The scores and sound files, where applicable, can be found at: homopromos.org/gay-century.html.

Please contact info@homopromos.org to discuss further.

*Peter Scott-Presland*
*2nd February 2021*

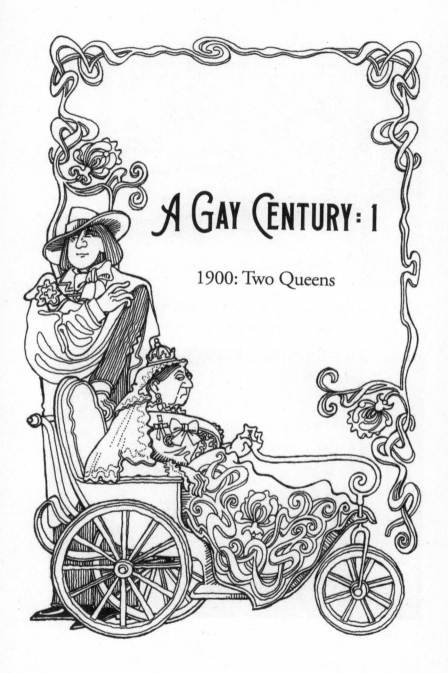

# A Gay Century: 1

## 1900: Two Queens

Above: *Oscar Wilde on his deathbed 1900 [Maurice Gilbert]*
Below: *Queen Victoria by Bertha Muller*

# INTRODUCTION

The story of gay life in the twentieth century – leaving aside a lot of people simply living, loving and enjoying themselves – is the story of an epic battle between repression and liberation. Add in, too, a strong dose of self-oppression, because much of the struggle on the part of Gay Rights activists was against other gay people: the struggle to convince them that they *deserved* rights. So where better to start with the icon, Queen Victoria, pitted against the prophet of self-expression and self-fulfilment, Oscar Wilde?

It is 30th November 1900, in a small bedroom at the dingy Hotel d'Alsace in Paris. The Angel of Death is hovering over Wilde, and he is on the point of departure from this life, when Queen Victoria appears in the room. She is less than two months away from her own death: 81 and enormously fat. [She had a 50-inch waist, judging from the pair of her bloomers which survive in the V & A.] She was also blind.

Against the historical evidence, we allow Victoria to walk a little in this piece, to make it more visual, and because it is fantasy, most of the other details used in this piece are true.

Researching the piece, I was struck, as I did not expect to be, by similarities between her and Wilde. Both were outsiders in their society. Victoria's first language was German, which was spoken in the Royal Household in private, and she retained a German accent; she was brought up in isolation, married a German, had few intimate friends. Wilde was an Irish parvenu who got rid of his accent to further his career.

Both infected their families – Victoria with haemophilia and Wilde with syphilis. Both adored sex. Despite this enthusiasm, Victoria has become a byword for prudishness, humourlessness, and censorship. This was the legacy bequeathed her by her overbearing and manipulative husband, Prince Albert. She was also distinctly iffy about the consequences of sex, i.e. children.

So the two Queens square up to each other. Because the viewpoint is Wilde's, Victoria is, of course, Lady Bracknell. Repression vs liberation – let battle commence!

Sources: *Victoria a Life* by AN Wilson [Atlantic Books 2015]
*Queen Victoria: A personal history* by Christopher Hibbert [Harper Collins 2001]
*Oscar Wilde* by Richard Ellman [Penguin 1988]
*The Stranger Wilde* by Gary Schmidgall [Dutton 1994]
*The Secret Life of Oscar Wilde* by Neil McKenna [Arrow 2004]

CAST

**QUEEN VICTORIA :** Contralto (or possibly male alto)
*81 years old. Very small and enormously fat. She suffers from chronic arthritis and uses a bath chair. Her German accent becomes pronounced when she is worked up.*

**OSCAR WILDE :** Baritone
*46 years old, very tall, and running to fat. Longish hair. His ear is bandaged [it is very painful after unsuccessful surgery]. Strong English accent, which slips into his native Dublin when he is agitated.*

**PAGE :** Non-speaking/singing
*Queen Victoria's attendant – dressed as for court.*

SETTING

30th November 1900.

Oscar Wilde's room at the Hotel d'Alsace; sparsely furnished, an old bed, a bedside table. His overcoat is used as a bedspread.

INSTRUMENTS

Piano, Flute, Violin, Cello

# TWO QUEENS

*[A short musical prologue. As the lights slowly come up, they reveal the room is sparsely furnished; an old bed, a bedside table.*

*Wilde is lying in bed on his back, dying. His mouth is wide open, his breathing is laboured and heavy.*

*Attended by a page boy carrying a small hand-bell and a tin, VICTORIA appears suddenly at the doorway, in her bath chair. Her reticule is in her lap, a walking stick tucked in at her side.]*

VICTORIA:     Mr Wilde! Mr Wilde!

*[The PAGE pushes her part-way into the room.]*

> Rise, sir, from that recumbent posture.

*[WILDE wakes. He is very groggy, disorientated. The PAGE moves VICTORIA closer to the bed side. He fusses over her before placing the hand bell and tin in her lap. From his pocket he produces an embroidered napkin and tucks it into her collar, smoothing it out down her front.*

*WILDE clears his throat, coughing and 'phlegmy'.]*

WILDE:        Where's Robbie? Where's Reggie?

*[VICTORIA dismisses the PAGE, who leaves, closing the door behind him. WILDE becomes more lucid and aware that he is not alone.]*

VICTORIA:     Your young friends have gone.
                      Everyone's gone.

[*WILDE realises who it is; he struggles to rise…*]

WILDE:        Majesty! It is a signal honour.

[*…but fails and collapses to a seated position on the bed.*]

VICTORIA:     We heard of your parlous state.
                      Your poverty, your operation…
                      How is your poor ear?

WILDE:        I bear it with what fortitude I can,
                      Having had some abatement.
                      I have been out in a carriage with my
                          friends.

VICTORIA:     We hope you have been behaving very well.

WILDE:        I have not been feeling very well.

VICTORIA:     In that case you very likely have.
                      Behaving well and feeling well rarely go
                          together.

WILDE:        I am dying, Majesty.

VICTORIA:     And have been for some weeks.
                      We really think it is high time

That you made up your mind,
Whether you are going to live or to die.
This shilly-shallying with the question is
    absurd.

WILDE: The doctor says I cannot live.

VICTORIA: Then we hope that you will act
On his medical advice.
Our doctors say much the same,
And we intend to follow
Their guidance unquestioningly.
*[Pensive]* We shall not be long after you.

*[Her mood brightens.]*

You had the last rites, we believe.

WILDE: Oh yes. It was a comfort
When the Catholic Church received me in.

VICTORIA: We are glad to hear it.
A man should always have an occupation
Of some kind.

*[He struggles to get out of bed.]*

WILDE: I will not live out the century.
The English people would not stand for it.

*[Having failed to stand, he sits on the edge of the bed, trying to put his shoes on.]*

VICTORIA:     No need for shoes for you now!

*[He throws the shoes aside.]*

WILDE:     Do you have any cigarettes?

VICTORIA:     Certainly not. We only smoke opiates.

WILDE:     Perhaps a glass of absinthe?

VICTORIA:     Mr Wilde, absinthe is a drink
              For Bohemians and anarchists.
              It is not a fitting beverage for a queen.

*[WILDE double-takes the audience. VICTORIA rummages under her voluminous skirts and brings out a hip flask.]*

VICTORIA:     You may partake of this.

*[She passes the flask to WILDE who takes it somewhat dubiously.]*

              Just a little, mind –

*[He removes the stopper and sniffs the contents.]*

              A cocktail of claret, scotch and laudanum –

We swear by it.
We never go anywhere without it.

*[He takes a drink and finds it to his liking. VICTORIA has another rummage and produces a cream cake. She appears childishly happy.]*

VICTORIA:    Mr Wilde,
We heard how you honoured us
On our Diamond Jubilee –
A party for the children of Berneval.

*[She bites the cake greedily, cream goes round her mouth as she bolts it.]*

WILDE:    I love children.
I have not seen my own for six years –
I miss them dreadfully.

VICTORIA:    Children are the price one pays
For the pleasures of congress.
Sometimes we look at ours
And ask if it was worth it.

*[She speaks/sings through another greedy bite.]*

Look what childbirth has done to our
figure.

*[She picks up the handbell and rings it delicately.]*

WILDE:          Children are an avoidable pleasure.

*[The PAGE enters with a folded cloth over his arm and respect-fully cleans around her mouth.]*

VICTORIA:       *[She splutters]* Mr Wilde!
                Do you imagine
                That we would form an alliance
                With a prophylactic?

*[The PAGE picks up the cake, removes the napkin; he attempts to remove the tin but she holds on to it. She waves the PAGE away; he leaves.]*

WILDE:          You are right. Majesty
                One should never avoid a pleasure

VICTORIA:       And it was a pleasure.
                Such a pleasure.
                *[She sighs]* Oh Albert.

WILDE:          Ah yes! My party in your honour…
                I invited local schoolboys in Berneval,
                And their teacher, Monsieur Hossein,
                And the postman, and the curé –
                All devoted to your Majesty.
                There were union flags,
                The little children sang the Marseillaise,
                And then God Save the Queen.

VICTORIA:    How charming!

*[She brightens suddenly]*

We hear you had a giant cake…

BOTH:        …With *Jubilé de la reine Victoria*…

WILDE:       …Iced in pink and green.

*[VICTORIA opens her tin and pulls out a chocolate.]*

VICTORIA:    We love cake!
             Did you have chocolates too?

*[She attempts to bite the chocolate but fails, it is too hard. She replaces it and closes the tin.]*

WILDE:       Yes, and grenadine,
             And strawberries and cream.

VICTORIA:    Cream too! We love cream.
             Chocolate, cake and cream –
             You seem to have lived entirely for pleasure.

WILDE:       Pleasure has been my downfall.

VICTORIA:    Mr Wilde, tell us frankly:
             Was it true, what was said at your trials?

WILDE:     I denied it always.

VICTORIA:  That was not what we asked.
           To lose one trial may be regarded as a mis-
               fortune,
           To lose three seems like carelessness.
           *[Pointed]* Or guiltiness.

WILDE:     Well, your majesty, I must confess,
           Beauty in all its forms
           Has always attracted me.

VICTORIA:  You need not be so mealy-mouthed.
           We have read Krafft-Ebing.
           You mean you are bisexual?

WILDE:     Yes, your majesty.

VICTORIA:  Oh, they count as heterosexuals,
           They dine with us.
           Or come in the evening at any rate.

WILDE:     You are too kind.

VICTORIA:  We cannot say that we approve of you.
           You lavished too much mockery
           Upon society, and that is vulgar.
           Never speak disrespectfully of society;
           Only people who can't get into it do that.

Mr Wilde, it may surprise you, but we like
  you.
According to our son, Bertie,
You are the greatest wit in Europe.

WILDE:      I was the greatest wit...

VICTORIA:    He came ...

WILDE:      Was...

VICTORIA:    ...to all your opening nights,
And laughed immoderately.

WILDE:      What a talent once I had!
All is gone.

VICTORIA:    We read your plays as they were published.
We do so like to be amused.

WILDE:      But I am nothing with no audience.
So what is left but a long, slow,
Long slow, lovely suicide?

VICTORIA:    We have been in secret
Paying you a pension
These last few years,
In thanks for our enjoyment.
It is nothing short of scandal
That you should be treated so.

WILDE:       Oh, hypocrisy!

VICTORIA:    Why? Have you been leading a double life,
             Pretending to be wicked
             And being really good all the time?
             Now, *that* would be hypocrisy.

WILDE:       You say that you admire my work?
             What then has my private life to do with
                 that?
             You punish me, not for what I do,
             But for what I am.

VICTORIA:    We punish no-one.
             The law, the judge, the juries
             Punish you.

WILDE:       You made the law, your majesty,
             That caused my downfall.

VICTORIA:    I, sir?
             What has it to do with me?

WILDE:       You signed it into law.
             You could have stopped it.
             You condemned me to a life of shame –

VICTORIA:    Shame that you found thoroughly
                 becoming:
             All those secrets, all those masks.

Your work thrived on it.
You would not have had it any other way.

WILDE: *[Anguished]* Not only me, many others.
Poor Francis Douglas, my Bosie's brother,
Shot himself the day after he was engaged,
Because of rumours of a liaison
With your Prime Minister, Rosebery,
Of whom you were so fond.

VICTORIA: *[She is lost in her memories.]* We were.
We used to mother him,
Tell him he should wrap up warm.

WILDE: And what about your own beloved grandson,
Prince Eddie?

VICTORIA: What of him?

WILDE: Because you did not stand up to Gladstone
And let that legislation pass,
You almost ruined your own family.

VICTORIA: We know not what you mean –

WILDE: Does the Cleveland Street scandal
Mean nothing to you?
The favours of telegraph boys…

VICTORIA: A baseless allegation of the Press;

Fake news of a radical persuasion.

WILDE:        I was in France in Ninety-One.
              Your grandson had been there nine months
                  before,
              And very red he was
              At some of the reporters' questions.
              French journalists know everything
              About our royalty,
              More than we do ourselves.
              It is a form of envy.

VICTORIA:     *[VICTORIA, in anguish, resorts to her native
                  German accent.]*
              Ach! Du Englisch!

WILDE:        *[Angry]* I am not English! Irish, Majesty.

VICTORIA:     You are obsessed with finding fault,
              Und schniffing shcandal.

WILDE:        I am an Irish gentleman.

VICTORIA:     *[She calmly returns to English.]*
              You may be Irish, sir, but you are no gentle-
                  man.
              You forfeited the right to be called 'gentle-
                  man'
              When you gave your poor wife
              The French disease.

WILDE:      A baseless rumour –

VICTORIA:   On this point, as on all points, we are firm.

WILDE:      Even if true, is that worse
            Than giving your son and grandsons
            Haemophilia?

*[He points in accusation; VICTORIA quails.]*

VICTORIA:   How were we to know?

WILDE:      And how was I to know?
            I thought that I was cured.

*[The lighting grows dimmer and both seem to fade in private thoughts. The PAGE enters carrying lit candles which he places on the side table, brightening the room. He ensures VICTORIA is comfortable, then leaves.]*

WILDE:      Blighted...
            Prince Leopold, your youngest child,
            Your grandson, Prince Friedrich –
            Only three years old.
            There will be more...
            ...Many more.
            You have spread your fatal curse
            Across the whole of Europe.
            There will not be a royal house
            From Spain to Russia

28

That will be free of your tainted blood.

VICTORIA: *[In tears]* We did not know.
How could we know?

WILDE: Your doctors should have known.

VICTORIA: They did not tell us if they did.
We did not know.

WILDE: Well, you know now.

VICTORIA: Yes, we know now.
*[Icy]* Thank you, Mr. Wilde

*[VICTORIA pulls herself together. She fumbles in her lap for her reticule… which she accidently knocks to the floor. WILDE picks it up and holds it out to her. She ignores him, fumbling still. At this moment, WILDE realises that VICTORIA is blind. It softens him. In a panic she grabs her bell and rings it madly. The PAGE enters quickly. Seeing the reticule in WILDE's hand, he takes it from WILDE, then reaches for VICTORIA's hand, giving it to her.*

*VICTORIA is visibly relieved, and opens the reticule, takes out a handkerchief, dabs her eyes and mouth, then returns it to the reticule.]*

WILDE: Forgive me, Majesty.

*[WILDE, rather theatrically, goes down on one knee. He takes her hand and places it on his head. She pulls her hand away sharply. WILDE loses his balance, and falls over.]*

VICTORIA:     Mr Wilde, if you think we are going to
                knight you,
            You are very much mistaken –
            Much though you desired it.

*[He raises himself to a sitting position...]*

VICTORIA:     Well, we will forgive you.
            You have a blazing cheek –
            Which is half of your function
            And all of your charm.

            Do you recall, you had the nerve
            To ask us for a poem
            To feature in some magazine?

WILDE:        'The Woman's World'…

*[She turns abruptly to face WILDE accusingly]*

VICTORIA:     We, who could never in our whole life
            Write one line of verse,
            Serious or comic,
            Or even make a rhyme!

But we were flattered to be asked.
We never showed it, but we were,
And we liked 'The Woman's World',
Especially when your Mother wrote of us.

*[The PAGE fusses, making her comfortable.]*

WILDE:      Do you remember when we met?

VICTORIA:   We met so many...

WILDE:      You were a ruby set in jet;
            Such a regal walk,

*[VICTORIA, now much more relaxed, dismisses the PAGE, who leaves.]*

VICTORIA:   No walking now for us.

*[It is WILDE's turn to become agitated.]*

WILDE:      I was unjust.
            It was not you who sealed my fate,
            It was many things.
            Most of all I blame myself.

VICTORIA:   We blame that awful Henry Labouchère

WILDE:      Labouchère...

BOTH: Nothing but trouble.

VICTORIA: And nothing less than a Republican!

WILDE: *[Nods in agreement]* A mischief-maker!

VICTORIA: He wanted to convert the Palace
Into a home for fallen women!

WILDE: Yes, a trouble maker!
You kept him from the Cabinet.
Gladstone wanted him, but you refused.
Yet you could not refuse that vicious clause,
Sneaked into law when nobody was
looking.

VICTORIA: Please don't start all that again.

WILDE: He was of course an atheist.
When you deprive yourself of God,
You have to play yourself at being one.

VICTORIA: Mr Wilde, we have not much time –
We have to go and plan our funeral.
The elements are all in place,
But we want some touches,
Personal mementos in the coffin.
Oh, how we love a proper funeral!

WILDE: I fear a pauper's grave for me.

VICTORIA: You do not plan your funeral?
For men it is different;
A funeral should come on a man as a surprise,
Pleasant or unpleasant, as the case may be.
It is hardly a matter
He can be allowed to arrange himself.

We strongly advise that you have a haircut.
Locks of hair make tasteful funeral gifts
When arranged in pretty lockets

WILDE: I fear, that I am beyond arranging anything.

VICTORIA: Quite right, for you are dead,
And we must go.
Strange to think we have so much in common.

BOTH: We were both outsiders.

VICTORIA: We alone with our hundred dolls
In Kensington.

WILDE: I, prancing around
The snobbish paddocks
Of high society.
I worked hard to lose my accent –

VICTORIA:    We never needed to –
             Because we were the Queen.
             Geliebte Volksmutter.

*[The PAGE reappears to tidy up and put out the candles.]*

VICTORIA:    May we prevail upon you, Mr. Wilde,
             To push our bath chair?

WILDE:       Certainly, Majesty.

VICTORIA:    You know, Mr Wilde,
             We are but thirty-two days away
             From the Twentieth Century.

WILDE:       I wonder what that century
             Will make of us.

BOTH:        We will of course be two
             Of the most famous figures
             Of this one.
             And two of the most recognisable.

VICTORIA:    We will stand for something.
             Order. Stability. Empire.
             Loyalty.

WILDE:       Hypocrisy

VICTORIA:    Morality

WILDE:          Prudery. Repression.
                Victorian values.
                A stick to beat my kind
                Down the ages.

VICTORIA:       But we were not like that.

WILDE:          And I will stand for Art:
                The rights of Artists,
                And for courage
                In the face of persecution.

VICTORIA:       Irresponsibility, dissipation,
                Depravity, shallowness,
                Luxury and unreliability.

WILDE:          But I am not like that.

*[He goes to the bed, picks up his coat, shakes it out then puts it on.]*

VICTORIA:       We do not say you are,
                But so you will seem.

*[He returns to push the bath chair. They move towards the front of the stage.]*

BOTH:           We are neither what we seem,
                But what we seem is what is useful
                To set the coming century's theme,
                More convenient than truthful.

*[WILDE faces VICTORIA.]*

WILDE:        I was right, it is a world of masks.

VICTORIA:     We wore one just as much as you.

WILDE:        But I used mine to tell the truth.

VICTORIA:     While on ours the canker grew,
              So we were trapped in ours.

*[VICTORIA seems to have no further need of her bath chair. She stands up, without the need for her stick, and takes his arm. They come to the foot of the stage, forming a tableau for the audience.]*

BOTH:         So here we are, each behind our mask,
              And you will take our mask.
              You will not want to ask
              About a truth that's complicated by
              The lie that tells the truth that's yet a lie.

*[They turn and promenade, as the PAGE opens the door.]*

              And as we disappear into the past,
              You will not hear us say 'Goodbye'.
              For we are always with you,
              Clichés oh so ripe,
              Full-blooded stereotype,

*[They are in the doorway.]*

Nature's opposites.
And on our shoulders sits
The battle of the twentieth century –
Two fat old queens.

VICTORIA:    We throw our good fat weight
Upon the scales of decency.

WILDE:    I use my wit to arm
The liberation of identity.

BOTH:    We are twin pillars
Of the century.
You have to choose a side
In the twentieth century.

*[They move backwards into oblivion as the door slowly closes.]*

SLOW FADE TO BLACKOUT

THE END

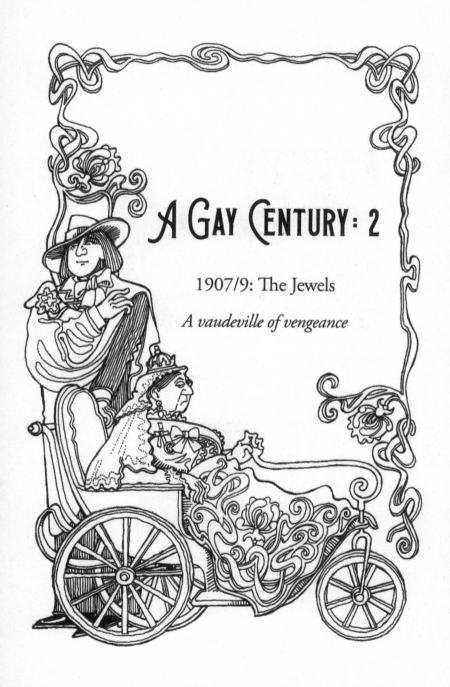

# A Gay Century: 2

## 1907/9: The Jewels

*A vaudeville of vengeance*

Above Left: *Sir Arthur Vicars, KCVO: Ulster King of Arms*

Above Right: *Frank Shackleton in Boer War*

Below: *Irish Crown Jewels, stolen June 1907*

# INTRODUCTION

*A* new century, a new monarch, but memories of the old century linger on. Edward VII is far more homophobic than his mother Victoria, who had a particular fondness and friendship for effeminate/homosexual/kinky men. Her first Prime Minister, whom she was so infatuated with that there were rumours of marriage, had a fondness for spanking; her later favourites were the flamboyant Disraeli, whose companionate marriage may have masked homosexual feelings, and the Earl of Rosebery, whose affair with Lord Alfred Douglas's brother led to the poor boy's suicide. Victoria mothered him rotten, and told him to wrap up warm when he went out in winter.

Among her favourites were Lord Ronald Gower [pronounced 'Gaur'], who appears here. He was one of the very few non-family members she called by their first name. Gower, ten years older than Wilde, was extremely well connected – four of his sisters married Dukes. Bertie, Victoria's eldest son, couldn't stand him, accused him of unnatural practices, but was forced to withdraw the accusation under the threat of a court case. Gower subsequently fled the country at the time of the Cleveland Street scandal which embroiled Victoria's eldest grandson, Bertie's son Victor Albert.

Gower's practices are somewhat mysterious, but John Addington Symonds, a gay rights pioneer, accused him of *'urningthum [homosexuality] of the rankest, most diabolical kind*'. Symonds himself had a dogged devotion to a Venetian gondolier, so it may be simply a reference to a penchant for casual sex. Or it may be something more in the sado-masochistic line. Either way, he gathered round himself a gay circle, a community, which was defiantly active while society was still reeling from the Labouchère amendment, Cleveland Street, and the Wilde trials.

This is relevant, because another of our characters, Frank Shackleton, was an extremely attractive piece of totty who would shag anyone, of any gender, if he could get anything out of it. His one redeeming feature was his devotion to his brother, the polar explorer Ernest Shackleton, for whom he tried to raise money.

Frank Shackleton has been described as a 'go-between' between Dublin Castle and Lord Ronald. Why they should need a go-between historians have not paused to enquire. My guess is that promising Irish lads were given an introduction to London queens, with Frank vouching that they were not blackmailers. In return he brought back gossip, especially court gossip, and possibly money.

The historians who have written about the case show remarkably little knowledge of, or interest in, the way gay society works.

And so to the case itself. 'Irish Crown Jewels' was the rather grandiose name given to a couple of nondescript cast-offs from William IV, which were nevertheless worth a few million in today's money. They were kept in Dublin Castle under the guardianship of Sir Arthur Vicars, Ulster King of Arms, an alcoholic queen who was potty about heraldry. Largely self-taught, he loved it for the opportunities it gave him to dress up, and to invent rituals which made him important.

There had been a gay scandal in Dublin Castle in 1884 – one of the people involved was Jack Saul, who also turns up in Cleveland Street, and authored a major work of Victorian gay porn, *The Sins of the Cities of the Plain*. Vicars kept the gay tradition alive and well by appointing other nancies to such invented positions as Athlone Pursuivant, Cork Herald, and Dublin Herald (a post filled by Frank Shackleton).

In 1907 Vicars contrived to lose the jewels, and they have never been recovered. It was a time of fervent nationalism, and anti-nationalism, and to this day various motives are ascribed to the thieves. Edward VII demanded they be caught, there was an incompetent investigation which was abruptly halted, probably when it appeared that it might turn up scandal which would implicate the Royal Household – yet again.

For Edward VII this was particularly galling because England was not the only country buzzing with gay scandal. The court of his nephew Wilhelm had been blown apart two years previously by a libel case which led to a series of resignations from the German Court. In this trial, it was revealed that one of the Kaiser's close chums, Prince Eulenberg, and his lover the military commander of Berlin, were both in the habit of calling the Kaiser *liebchen [darling]*. This brought a blistering ticking off from Edward about the importance of keeping the imperial nose clean. Imagine the Kaiser's glee when his overbearing uncle was seen to be equally compromised. Pots and kettles? Cue howls of Hunnish laughter.

And yet, when it comes down to it, nobody knows who stole the jewels, why they stole the jewels, what became of the jewels, why the investigation of the theft was so cack-handed, or why it was called off. When the whole outline of what actually happened is so hazy and contested, art can slip in through the cracks, and may even contain the germ of truth.

Following the rather stately and formal *Prologue*, which lays out the parameters of the whole cycle, I wanted a strong contrast in the way of pace and variety. Much of *The Jewels* is, frankly, silly, because the whole case is silly. I have used more rhyme and formal versification, and describe it as a vaudeville. It has strong elements of commedia dell' arte and silent film, with Keystone Cop chases and absurd props (sausages for the Crown Jewels). I could imagine it performed on the stage of Dan Lowry's Palace of Varieties in Dublin.

I also hope it brings to the case of poor wronged Oscar a kind of poetic justice. The spirit of Oscar will linger through the cycle, as will the ghost of Victoria.

Sources:    *Scandal & betrayal: Shackleton and the Irish crown jewels* by John Cafferky and Kevin Hannafin [Collins 2002]
*Vicious Circle: The Case of the Missing Irish Crown Jewels* by Frances Bamford and Viola Bankes [Horizon Press 1967]
https://web.archive.org/web/20130511165435/
http://www.nationalarchives.ie/digital-resources/
online-exhibitions/the-theft-of-the-irish-
%E2%80%9Ccrown-jewels%E2%80%9D-2007/

# CAST

**SIR ARTHUR VICARS** : Bass-Baritone
*45 yrs old. A silly, fussy, self-important queen with a liking for dressing up;* doubles with *Edward VII, 66, fat, bearded, booming but petulant. Accustomed to getting his own way.*

**LORD RONALD GOWER** : Mezzo
*64 yrs old. A dreamy, otherworldly but very rich queen;* doubles with

**POLICEMAN – SERVANT – ENGLISH PAWNBROKER – FRENCH PAWNBROKER** [The extent of his doubling is a running joke.]

**FRANK SHACKLETON** : Tenor
*26 yrs old. Very slim, suave and handsome. Will shag anything that moves. Unscrupulous exploiter of gay men and older women.*

**BALLADEER** : Baritone
*Any age. Will tell the story in verse while accompanying himself on an Irish instrument (e.g. a hand-held harp, a guitar, an accordion)* doubles with

**ROBERT ROSS,** *39, plump, balding, good dresser. Well organised. Iron will beneath campy manner.*

**CAPTAIN GORGES** : Non-singing
*33 yrs old. A wild flaming dangerous man with a quick temper and no scruples. Doubles with*

**INSPECTOR JOHN KANE : Bass**
*40-ish. Evenin' all.*

## SETTING

Bare stage; multiple scenes. The opera incorporates elements of vaudeville/circus, and of silent movies. Strong parodic melodrama, with moments of seriousness. Silent movies created by revolving wheel in front of spotlight, for flicker effect. A small table somewhere for props. A string of pantomime sausages are on it – the Irish Crown Jewels.

## INSTRUMENTS

Piano, violin

# THE JEWELS

## PART ONE

### Prologue

BALLADEER: Gather round while I sing you a story that's old,
Resolve you a mystery that's never been told,
How the Irish Crown Jewels were wafted away,
And nobody knows where they are to this day.

Some said they were stolen for personal gain;
Others said 'No, it was men of Sinn Fein',
Who'd show up the British, the gov'nment and crown,
The vice ring of nancies in old Dublin Town.

The Home Rulers said it was Carson[1] to blame,
Who'd led for the crown as he wrecked Oscar's name.
His Unionists plotted to scupper Home Rule,
With a drunken old Mary to use as a tool.

---

[1] Sir Edward Carson, prosecutor of Wilde and later founder of the paramilitary Ulster Volunteer Force.

In nineteen-oh-seven the Medieval Tower
Was home to some queers – what a terrible
    shower!
They spent their time groping in each
    other's knickers –
And Dublin's chief groper was Sir Arthur
    Vicars...

## Scene One

*[Enter VICARS, wearing very silly finery. He does a little skip-*
*ping dance, a kind of camp Morris. He has a feather duster in*
*his hand. Shades of Gilbert and Sullivan.]*

VICARS:      I love my job, I'm the Ulster King of Arms.
The Minister for Ireland saw my charms.
I could fashion ceremonials,
Impress these poor colonials,
And fill the Irish peasants with alarms.

*[He dusts the sausages on the table – the Irish Crown Jewels.]*

These are my pretty, oh so very pretty
    jewels,
Nothing but em'ralds on the star;
And sparklers – they're Brazilian –
Together worth a million –
They'd buy an awful lot of caviar.
Here is the Badge of the Head of the Order,
More lovely em'ralds set round the border.

Rubies in the centre –
Locked in here where none can enter,
Safe from any murderous marauder.

*[He plays with the sausages.]*

See how they glow,
Laid in a row;
See how they shine –
They're mine, all mine

*[He takes a glass of champagne from the table and drinks.]*

*[Villain music. Enter FRANK. Direct to audience:]*

FRANK:          Not so fast, my fine feathered fairy!
                Your pride is coming before a fall.
                When I'm through with you
                They'll make a splendid haul –
                Payment for the years
                At your beck and call,
                As Dublin Herald, junior,
                My status so much punier.
                All these years you made me strip you,
                Forced me – oh the shame! – to whip you.
                I didn't enjoy it at all.

VICARS:         A Royal visit!
                The king is coming,
                His gracious Maj!

I'll parade in my finery,
Wear my badge.
I'll have a pretty ritual –
Sure to astound,
Devised to make it fit you all –
And boss you all around.

The jewels, the jewels,
All there to see,
Though everyone's really
Looking at me.

*[He takes another drink. Continues drinking through FRANK's monologue, and caressing the sausages – possibly phallicly. His dance continues, but gets more and more unsteady.]*

FRANK:      Now these years will pay off,
Flattering the fairies in Dublin Castle.
There are so many,
Dancing in a daisy chain,
Tied up in the cellars –
The dungeons finally have a use again.
Hail, Sodom and Begorrah!

VICARS:      *[Interspersed with FRANK]*
I love my work,
I love my heraldry,
My pretty jewels,
My lovely castle,
With its lovely walls

And lovely – ooh! – dungeons!

*[He giggles at the idea of the dungeons.]*

FRANK:        I have wormed my way in
With fresh-faced country boys,
Pure and new in town,
Dazzled by the spectacle
And by the odd half crown.
I have sounded out the police,
A fine upstanding body –
Upstanding in every way,
And very obliging with their favours.
The best of boys and men I can reward
By taking them across the Irish Sea
To Lord Ronald Gower.

GOWER:      *(Popping round the corner – to audience,
camp, spoken]*
That's me in a beard!

FRANK:        Gower, son of the Duke of Sutherland.
His sisters married Dukes and Royalty.

*[GOWER raises his hat politely to the audience, exits.]*

I move in the highest circles
In that land across the sea.
Gower's such a generous man,
To me and to them,

And thus I shall advance
Through homosexual vice rings
Which form concentric circles.

*[FRANK slinks up behind VICARS, clutches him seductively.]*

FRANK:        You look ravishing in your uniform.
              I never could resist a uniform.
              Come have another –
              Drink deep, drink deep!

*[To audience:]*

              Soon I'll have him fast asleep.

*[To VICARS:]*

              My dear, you're looking quite worn out,
              You're working far too hard.
              You'll wear yourself to pieces
              If you're not on your guard.

              Won't you have a little lie down?

VICARS:       *[Drunk]* I want to dance! I want to dance!
                  Ah!

FRANK:        *[Suggestive, slapping his bottom]*
              Later I'll give you a little tie-down!

VICARS:        *[Giggles]* Ooh!

*[They dance a few steps before FRANK lays him down on the floor gently. Then 'villain music' again.]*

FRANK:        Sleep you well, my pretty.
              Now I can rob you,
              Rob you of your most precious burden...

*[Reaches into VICARS' pocket. VICARS responds in his sleep to the groping. FRANK produces the object he seeks in triumph. To audience:]*

              Your keys!

              I will not steal the jewels now –
              I need an alibi.
              I will have keys copied
              For my crony,
              Richard Gorges.
              I knew him in the Boer War.
              We were both cashiered
              From the Army,
              But Gorges is far worse than me.
              He raped a little drummer boy,
              Where I only seduced one...

              When I have the jewels
              I will pawn them,
              Pay off all my debts,

And give my brother
Ernest Shackleton –
Hero and explorer –
Enough to fund his dream,
His latest expedition
To the frozen far Antarctic.

*[Exits. A brief blackout in which VICARS gets up, places the sausages on a table, and lies down again.]*

Interlude

BALLADEER: Shackleton fled back to old London Town.
He left Richard Gorges to shake Vicars
down.
He crept to the Tower under cover of night,
While the Police *[pron. PO-lis]* who guard it
kept well out of sight.

*[Silent film. Flickering projector. GORGES comes in with the keys. He turns one elaborately in the strong room door. Encourages boos from the audience. Indicates the sleeping VICARS and puts his finger to his lips. Exaggerated caution as he steps over VICARS, elaborately looks left and right, takes another key to open the safe; gingerly reaches onto the table to take the sausages. Snatches them, steps back over VICARS. As he exits, a Dublin POLICEMAN pokes his head around the corner. GORGES kisses him passionately, drops him and exits. POLICEMAN disappears. VICARS awakes.]*

## Scene Two

VICARS:      Oh my head! My head!
I wish I were dead.
So low have I sunk –
I must stop getting drunk.
*[Sudden realisation.]*
The King! The King arrives today
On the Royal visit.
I must rehearse the Irish peers,
To greet him properly.

*[A comedy servant comes in and notices the bare table. Total shock. Mimes to VICARS that the jewels are missing. VICARS ignores him.]*

All their robes and finery
Must be totally correct;
His Majesty King Edward
Is a stickler for protocol,
Worse even than his mother.
It comes from living in her shadow.

*[The servant's mime gets more desperate and hysterical.]*

What is it? Not now.
I have affairs of state to think of.
I trust Lord Aberdeen has learnt his lines.
Tradition is so important –
That is why I invented this one.

*[The Servant is tugging his sleeve.]*

I said not now.

I've a stomach coming on;
This worry feeds my ulcer.

*[The Servant tugs again.]*

Whaaaaat?

*[The Servant points at the empty table. VICARS does a double take.]*

VICARS:     My jewels! My jewels!

*[He faints.]*

BLACKOUT

PART TWO

Prologue

*[The actions in the ballad are mimed to more silent film. EDWARD is a cartoon figure – pillow under shirt for stomach, obvious false beard, cardboard crown.]*

BALLADEER:  So Edward arrived, and he raged and he
roared
When he found that a burglar had stolen
his hoard.
He ordered the jewels to be found come
what may,
And given back quickly – he'd brook no
delay.

Silent film

*[EDWARD mimes instructions to JOHN KANE, of Scotland Yard. Keystone cops. KANE looks everywhere in speeded up motion. Searches the audience. Stops someone crossing the stage, makes him turn out his pockets, drop his trousers, cavity search etc – but comic. Enter FRANK and LORD GOWER.]*

Scene One

FRANK:  *[Spiv-like]* Want to buy some nice crown
jewels?

GOWER:       What would I do with crown jewels?

FRANK:       They're going cheap. Worth eighty grand,
             But to you – forty.
             You've got the money, you know you have.
             Look at that. Look at them shine,
             Gleam and glitter.

GOWER:       *[Tempted]* They could be mine…

FRANK:       Think of the revenge:
             All your life he has tormented you –
             Bertie, that pot-bellied profligate pig,
             Despised you, accused you,
             Roundly abused you.
             He said you misused
             And perverted his son.

GOWER:       He did! He was very rude.
             I had to slap his wrist.

FRANK:       He banished you from court –

GOWER:       His mama would not have done that;
             She called me 'Her dear Ronald'…

FRANK:       So get your own back.
             Have the Irish jewels….

[He dangles them before GOWER, who, mesmerised, reaches out his hand towards them. A whistle offstage makes them freeze.]

Silent film

[Enter police inspector, KANE, who initiates comic chase in circles round a bemused GOWER. FRANK flees offstage. Eventually KANE turns on GOWER, who puts up his hands in horror and flees off too. KANE pursues him.]

Scene Two

[Re-enter FRANK.]

FRANK:      Gower will not have the jewels;
He says they are too hot.
I must have cash, by hook or crook –
What choices have I got?

[PAWNBROKER enters.]

Ah! A pawnbroker, by his balls…
Tell me, good man,
What will you give for these?
Highly desirable,
Highly collectable,

[PAWNBROKER starts to examine them suspiciously.]

Totally legal and
Quite undetectable,
Leaving the deal
Quite unsuspectable:
For any enthusiast
Wholly delectable –

Silent Film

*[The PAWNBROKER starts to examine them with his eye-glass. The whistle goes off again. Silent film. Enter KANE as before. PAWNBROKER flees. Same chase rigmarole as before. Lights fade here on the chase, then come up on the BALLADEER.]*

Interlude

BALLADEER: Wherever he goes, Frank is feeling the
squeeze.
With Kane on his heels, each pawnbroker
flees.
As every day passes his deficit's mounting,
Despite all his twisting and shady account-
ing.
His numerous lovers conspiring to shun
him,
His numerous creditors eager to dun him.
Now the trap's closing, Frank hasn't a
chance
Unless he can cash in the jewels in France.

Scene Three

*[Dramatic change of music to cliché French accordion-style waltz. PAWNBROKER enters as before, with '3 balls' sign, and something like a baguette. He hangs the sign.]*

PAWNBROKER: *[To Audience, spoken:]*
C'est moi, c'est moi dans un beret. Je suis un autre – er – pawnbroker. Je porte cette baguette pour indiquer que je suis français. Vive la France! Hurrah!

*[Sung, turning to FRANK:]*

Zut alors ! Que voulez-vous ?

FRANK: Ah ! Bonjour !
J'ai ici dans mes actuel – er – hands
Les plus beaux – jewels – du monde.
Ils sont si – er – jolis que vous ne pouvez pas
Les refuser, je suis sur.

PAWNBROKER: Mon dieu!
Mais ceux sont les plus rares specimens
Des – emeralds – braziliennes
Si je ne suis pas – mistaken –
Voila les célèbres – Irish –
Crown Jewels –

Que tu as – stolen – du château de
Dublin.

FRANK:     Merde!

PAWNBROKER:   Je vous donnerai pour ces – jewels –
Er – mille francs!

FRANK:     Mille francs!

*[He looks in a little phrase book.]*

A THOUSAND?!
Je ne peux pas – er – buy –
Even un petit déjeuner
Avec mille francs!
Cinq million francs!

PAWNBROKER:   Cinq milles francs!

FRANK:     Deux million?

PAWNBROKER:   Deux milles! Deux milles!
Deux milles frances!

FRANK:     Cinq million! Cinq million!
Cinq million francs!

*[A lot of gesturing with numbers; possible duet round numbers
and mille/million.]*

FRANK:        Ma foi!
              Vous avez le – er – cheek – du diable.
              Ce n'est pas assez d'argent
              Pour payer le prix
              D'un – er – return ticket to Paris.
              Même le – er – clasp – est worth plus que ça.

PAWNBROKER:   Comme tu veux.
              Ce n'est pas le skin off mon nez.
              Et bien – vingt mille francs !
              C'est offer finale.
              Si tu n'accepteras pas mon offer,
              Tu peux sticker les jewels
              Dans ton – er – arse.

FRANK:        Je n'ai pas de – er – choice ;
              Tu m'as vraiment sur un – er – barrel.

PAWNBROKER:   Exactement.

*[He offers his hand.]*

BOTH:         *[To audience:]* I hate foreigners.

Silent film

*[They are about to shake hands, but there is a whistle off-stage. Silent film again. KANE enters, chases FRANK, who throws the sausages to PAWNBROKER, KANE follows the sausages, which are thrown back. Characters freeze.]*

Scene Four

*[Lights change from silent film. Sudden change of music to funeral procession. Enter ROBERT ROSS pulling a cart, on which is a large teddy bear laid on top of a rich velvet cloth. It is the corpse of Oscar Wilde.]*

ROSS:          I cleared Oscar's debts,
His bankruptcy discharged,
Thanks to German royalties
From Richard Strauss.
The opera *Salome* is decadent,
But in German sounds quite respectable.
So Oscar says farewell now to
*L'Enterrement de sixième classe*
*Au cimetière parisien de Batignolles.*

No more the obscurity
Of a suburban grave.
You are going now where you belong,
To Père Lachaise,
Among the immortals of the arts –
Chopin, Molière and La Fontaine,
Bizet, Balzac, Beaumarchais.
And now, in Division Eighty-Nine
On Avenue Carette,
Oscar Wilde.
No Bosie here today;
Oscar is all mine now,
And soon we'll have

A fine memorial.

'And alien tears will fill for him
Pity's long-broken urn,
For his mourners will be outcast men,
And outcasts always mourn.'
Bad poetry, but a fine epitaph.

*[To the Teddy Bear:]*

Not long now, Oscar.
Soon you can sleep in peace.

Silent Film

*[Abrupt change to silent film music again. The chase unfreezes.
Continues around ROSS and Oscar. Sausages continue to change
hands back and forth. As KANE finally collars FRANK, he slips
the sausages to ROSS, who double takes the audience, then slides
them under the bear. Lights change back from silent film. Music
change to funereal again. ROSS slowly pushes the cart past the
PAWNBROKER, FRANK and KANE, who take off their hats
and bow their heads in respect. Break of mood as ROSS exits.]*

Scene Five

KANE:        All right. Where are they?

FRANK:       Where are what?

KANE:        The jewels, the royal jewels.

FRANK:       Which jewels might those be?

KANE:        You know the jewels I mean.
             The Irish Jewels,
             Nicked from Dublin Castle
             Two years ago.

FRANK:       Oh yes! I think I read
             About it at the time.
             I was in London I believe.

KANE:        I have tracked you half across Europe
             To every pawnbroker you visited.
             Why did you go to all those pawnbrokers,
             If not to pawn the jewels?
             But everyone refused you,
             They were too hot.

FRANK:       If I have the jewels, where are they?
             You can search me.

KANE:        I intend to. Stretch your arms
             And spread.

*[FRANK does so. KANE pats him down thoroughly. FRANK is
ticklish. Comic business with search of inside leg and crotch area.
KANE is astonished at the size of FRANK's member, and conveys
this to the audience.]*

FRANK:      Satisfied?

KANE:       You must have them somewhere –
            You have hidden them.

FRANK:      I have a perfect alibi for the theft.

KANE:       Frank Shackleton, I arrest you
            On suspicion of robbery...

FRANK:      *[Intertwining]* I am innocent.
            I never stole the jewels,
            I was in London.
            Ask my friends –
            Ask Lord Ronald Gower.
            This is an outrage!
            An outrage!
            I demand the right of law!
            Call my solicitor now –
            Call Lord Ronald Gower!

KANE:       *[Together]* ...In that you did take
            The Star and the Badge
            Of the Grand Master
            Of the Order of Saint Patrick,
            Known as the Irish Crown Jewels.
            I must warn you
            That anything you say
            May be taken down
            And used against you.

*[KANE puts FRANK in handcuffs and takes him off. The singing continues offstage.]*

FRANK:      You have no evidence –

KANE:      I'll get the evidence –

FRANK:      No jewels – no proof – no charge –

KANE:      I'll break you yet!

EACH TO OTHER:   YOU SWINE!

BLACKOUT

PART THREE

Scene One

*[EDWARD VII again. He is in a terrible, petulant temper.]*

EDWARD:     Two years and still no jewels!
                What a disgrace! Two years!
                Why do I have policemen?

*[To audience:]*

They *are* mine, too:
'His Majesty's Inspectorate of Constabulary' –
See? 'His Majesty' – that's me!
His Majesty's Prisons too!
Mine, all mine!
And I want *my* police
To find the thief of *my* jewels;
I want him tried in *my* court
By *my* judges,
To go to *my* prison.

Where is that fool Kane?
I put him on the job
Two years ago.
I told him, 'Leave no stone unturned.'
But I hear nothing.
He digs up nothing.
It's not fair –

I want my jewels!

KANE: *[Offstage]* Your majesty! Your majesty!

*[KANE appears hauling on FRANK by the collar. He drags him to EDWARD. He bows deeply and leaves them.]*

EDWARD: So you are the villain who stole my jewels!

FRANK: How could I, majesty?
I was far away
Across the Irish Sea,
Here in London,
With my good friend
Lord Ronald Gower.

EDWARD: That name again!

GOWER: *[To audience, head round the corner:]* Yes, me again!

EDWARD: He goads me everywhere,
A gaudy, giddy, galling gadfly.

GOWER: Wonderful alliteration! Well done!

EDWARD: *[To FRANK:]* You stayed with that notorious sodomite —

GOWER: How dare you! I am not a sodomite.

EDWARD:     You are too,
            Have been for forty years.


GOWER:      I'll sue the man who says so.


EDWARD:     You can't sue me, I am the king.
            So there! *[He sticks out his tongue.]*


FRANK:      Gentlemen, gentlemen –
            Truce, I say.
            *[To EDWARD:]*
            If you say I'm the thief, *sire [ironic]*
            There'll be hell to pay.
            All the scandals
            The Castle has known
            Splashed in the press –
            There'll be mud on the Throne.
            Your own appointee,
            Lord Aberdeen,
            Governor of Ireland,
            Oft has been seen
            In the perfumed purlieus
            Of Lord Ronald Gower,
            Overripe and wanton
            Behind his closet door.

            Then Aberdeen's son,
            The sickly Lord Haddo,
            Smothered by mother,
            A bit of a saddo.

All of them here,
And all of the sort
That belonged in the circle
Where Gower held court.

Then Lorne – we've referred to
Your brother-in-law –
Whose passions were stirred too
By boys that he saw.
He lingered awhile
To be fingered awhile –
And now in the court
He'll be fingered again,
With all other aristo
Lovers of men.

EDWARD:    Hold! Stay! This cannot be!

Scandal, more scandal,
Here, there and everywhere.
Wilde and Gower –
That infamous pair!
The Cleveland Street scandal –
Gower was there,
Along with Prince Albert,
My son and my heir,
Feckless and reckless
By Gower sucked in.

FRANK:    Perhaps you'd like to reword that;

There's many would laugh if they heard
that.

EDWARD:  Gower had to flee to France,
Everybody looked askance,
Gave my son a telling glance.

But Victor Albert, he was fortunate.
As his father I silenced and paid off
The gutter press that was importunate.
After that, they laid off.
No-one would ever have known.
Then Wilde had his trials,
Despite his denials,
And Gower had to take off
To hinder detection.
Though Albert Victor was dead,
There were many who said
He shared Lorne's – Aberdeen's –
Haddo's too – Gower's too –
And Wilde's ghastly predilection.

Gower and his queer companions
Twine round the House of Saxe-Coburg-
Gotha
Like Virginia creeper.
They will choke us all to death!

GOWER:  And serve you right as well! *[Exits]*

EDWARD:     This cannot be!
            The monarchy is tottering,
            The Irish on the verge
            Of insurrection. As always.
            Fenians lurk in every corner.
            Last thing I need
            Is sodomy in high places –
            Again.

FRANK:      And think of your little Willie –

EDWARD:     There's nothing little 'bout my –

FRANK:      Your nephew, Kaiser Wilhelm Two,
            Of Germany –
            You lectured him, remember?
            The homosexual scandals round his court,
            The libel cases and revelations,
            How his chief of staff called him 'Darling' –

EDWARD:     Disgraceful! I told him,
            It'll bring the Hohenzollerns down.
            Take an honest mistress, just like me –
            It's far, far safer.

FRANK:      And now see all your own scandals
            Exploding in your face – pouf!

EDWARD:     Pouf?

FRANK:      Pouf!
            Imagine how they'll laugh throughout Berlin.

EDWARD:     A laughing stock…
            Shackleton, I've changed my mind;
            You're free to go.
            I'll order Kane to drop all charges,
            This case is closed.
            If the jewels are lost,
            It is a small price to pay
            For the future of the monarchy
            And the British Empire.

*[He sings. FRANK stands to attention.]*

            'Land of Hope and Glory,
            Mother of the free.
            How shall we extol thee,
            Who are born of thee?'
            *[To audience:]*
            That's my song, you know.
            AC Benson wrote the words for me –
            The son of the Archbishop –

FRANK:      *[To audience:]* Another of the Mary-Anns.
            Truly we are everywhere.

            *[To EDWARD:]*
            Your majesty, perhaps a little *douceur*…
            In exchange for keeping quiet?

EDWARD:     Blackmail? Hush money?
            Don't push your luck, sonny.

BLACKOUT

PART FOUR

Scene One

*[Funereal music. We are at Père Lachaise cemetery. ROBBIE ROSS by the grave of Oscar, with WILDE the Teddy Bear still on the cart. He looks into the hole, then takes OSCAR off the cart and lays him reverently on/in the ground. He takes the 'jewels' thoughtfully and fingers them.]*

ROSS:       Pretty baubles
            And worth a great deal…
            Not that the money matters a jot.
            If I report it,
            Hand back the jewels,
            I'll be arrested likely as not.

            I <u>should</u> report it
            That would be the correct thing.
            I have always respected the law,
            Even as I ignored it.

            But if I reported it,
            I would doubtless be arrested.
            Invert and aesthete,
            Doubly detested.

            Notorious pederast
            Must be suspected;
            Part of the vice ring,

Only expected;
Gower and Wilde's friend,
Highly connected –
See where it all leads –
Quickly detected.

No!
They stay here,
Here where they belong –
Yes, where they belong!

These philistines owe you
For the loathing they show you.
Despised and rejected,
Your honour in tatters;
Now the future holds
The only fame that matters.

Why should you not have them,
These jewels, these baubles?
Some sort of recompense
For all the discontents...
You were royal in your presence,
A prince among peasants,
And so-called royals
Cower in your shadow.

You deserve everything,
They deserve nothing.
This would be just,

This would be vengeance.

Here let them slumber and never be found,
Sleeping with Oscar, safe underground.
Where in the world should the jewels have
    been,
Except by the side of the true Irish queen?

*[He places the 'jewels' on OSCAR's chest, and covers the corpse
with the velvet cloth. Kneels by its side, lost in thought or prayer.
Slow fade.]*

Epilogue

*[ROSS and the BALLADEER double, so the changeover should
be seen by the audience. ROSS rises from his knees, removes his
jacket and hat, puts on the BALLADEER's clothes, picks up the
guitar or whatever instrument he is playing. To Audience:]*

BALLADEER: Thus ends a tale of an impudent crime,
The whole world agog with the news at the
    time.
The jewels are still missing, they've never
    been found;
So they might as well lie in a hole in the
    ground.

The whale-like Edward soon passed away,
Poor Vicars was shot by the Kerry IRA;

Frank swindled Lord Gower for all that he'd
    got,
And served fifteen months for his dastardly
    plot…

*[Spoken]*    Frank is buried in Chichester under a false
name. On his tombstone it says 'He lived
for others'. Gorges, the man who actually
stole the jewels, shot a policeman in 1915
but got off with a sentence of twelve
years. He threw himself under a train at
Edgware Road station in the 1950s. One
member of his family commented, 'If he
had to commit suicide, the least he could
have done was use a respectable station,
like South Kensington.'

So when you're in Paris, go see Père
    Lachaise,
Visit the tomb where Wilde's dreaming
    these days.
Admire his memorial, perhaps lay a wreath,
Imagine poor Wilde with his jewels under-
    neath.
His beautiful Sphinx caused an outrage
    back then
His testicles flaunted his queerness again,
Till a gardener, a prude, in a fit of the
    vapours

Castrated him, just for a weight for his
     papers.
And now they're replaced – this is rather
     pathetic –
With an anodyne, plastic and tasteful pros-
     thetic.

QUARTET:      The Jewels, the Jewels
              Turned men into fools;
              You mock at your peril
              Any Uranian.
              Lacking all pity
              He'll rifle your kitty,
              And it too may meet with
              A fate subterranean.

              The Jewels, the Jewels
              Turn men into fools,
              The rare sort of treasure
              For which they fight duels.
              Ponder his lost genitalia,
              Think the royal regalia:
              Regalia – genitalia –
              Whichever you think of,
              You're thinking of Oscar's crown jewels.

BLACKOUT

THE END

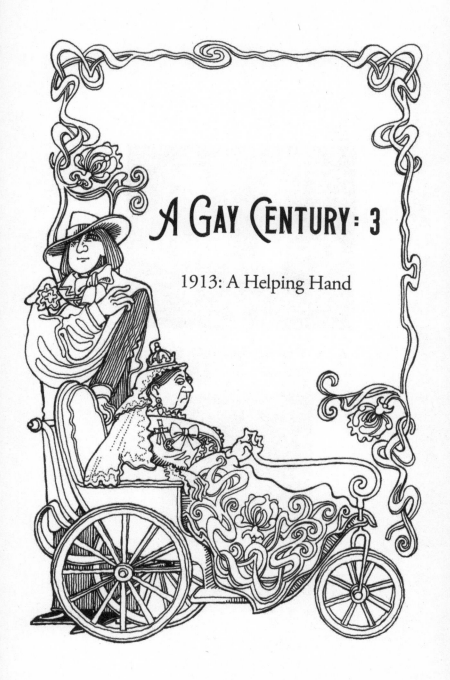

# A Gay Century: 3

## 1913: A Helping Hand

Above: *Edward Carpenter [left] and George Merrill c. 1900*
Below: *EM Forster portrait by Roger Fry 1911*

# INTRODUCTION

The genesis of EM Forster's queer novel *Maurice* is well known; Forster himself gives an account of it in his 1960 introduction to the novel, which still didn't appear until 1971, after his death. He describes a visit to the gay pioneer, Edward Carpenter, and his partner, George Merrill, in their farmhouse at Millthorpe, outside Sheffield. According to Forster, Merrill touched him on the buttocks, and the effect was such that a shock went through his body, and he instantly conceived (significant female term) the novel in its entirety.

Commentators have subsequently sexualised this encounter. According to that interpretation, Merrill was making a pass at Forster, and the sex-starved, love-starved Forster responded with a sexual utopian vision of an ideal relationship which cuts across the classes – crudely, an alliance with a pliable piece of rough trade. In that version the ever-closeted Forster had to dress up his rather obvious fantasy with pretentious philosophical trappings.

I have preferred to take Forster at his word, and evoke a golden late Edwardian summer afternoon, the kind of afternoon where you enter a dreamlike state, dopey with heat, and your mind floats away. Forster – Morgan to his friends – is a city man, itchy and sweating in a tweed three-piece suit, irritated by flies and annoyed at having to tramp the three miles from the station to the farm of his idol.

Edward Carpenter was an icon to Edwardian gays – a very public example of the possibility of gay relationships, and their acceptance in a community. A working class community, of course, because young working class men were always more relaxed about sex than the middle class. Also a community well away from any metropolis and the attentions of the police. Merrill was a fine example of that cheerful acceptance of sexuality – a self-educated man, very tactile, uninhibited in his expression of his needs and desires.

Merrill acted the role of the 'wife', cooking and cleaning, and ended up doing all the manual work in cottage and garden, mainly because Carpenter was crap at it. He had his fantasies about being a man of the soil and a manual worker, but his problem was that the sandals that he famously made were desperately uncomfortable. So Carpenter did his writing, thinking and public speaking while George looked after him; he also went with other boys, which George accepted until it looked as if one of them might take root. This might have been an exploitative relationship, but it worked and lasted for over thirty years.

For Forster, bullied since childhood at school and at home, lacking all confidence in himself as a sexual being, terrified of his mother, Carpenter and Merrill represented all he could aspire to, but would never find, or so he thought[2]. He had waited so long for this moment of meeting, and when it came, he found that the most potent thing he shared with Carpenter was an immersion in Indian philosophy and mysticism. This too feeds into the opera, and into his creativity – at the time he conceived *Maurice* he also received the germ of the idea for *A Passage to India*.

---

[2] He did realise his dream in part, with the bisexual policeman Bob Buckingham.

This opera presents the conception of *Maurice*, but music can express the multiple levels on which that takes place, and the true mystery of creation. About two-thirds through, Forster's fully formed thoughts are brought to life as he assumes the role of Maurice and George Merrill becomes Alec, and they sing their commitment to each other, with Carpenter insisting in the background that 'It has to have a happy ending'. It is a blurring of reality, creativity and sexual fantasy.

*A Helping Hand* is important in the cycle of *A Gay Century* because it represents the first glimmer of revival, of an idea of gay fulfilment in the face of the repression of the age. It will take several more operas to see that dream realised.

Sources:  *Maurice*, by EM Forster [Edward Arnold 1971]
*Concerning EM Forster* by Frank Kermode [Farrar, Straus and Giroux 2009]
*EM Forster, a life* by PN Furbank [Secker and Warburg 1979]
*Edward Carpenter, a life of liberty and love* by Sheila Rowbotham [Verso 2009]
*EM Forster* by Francis King [Thames and Hudson Literary Lives 1978]
*Edward Carpenter, an appreciation* ed. G Beith [George Allen 1931]
*A Visit to Gnani* by Edward Carpenter [Allen and Unwin 1911]
*My Days and Dreams* by Edward Carpenter [Allen and Unwin 1916]
*The Hill of Devi and other Indian Writings* by EM Forster [Edward Arnold 1983]

*Arctic Summer* by Damon Galgut [Atlantic 2014]
*The Dear Love of Comrades* by Noël Greig [Gay
Men's Press 1981]

## CAST

**EM FORSTER/MAURICE :** Tenor

*34, a townie, in uncomfortable suit, buttoned up and repressed. His moustache gives no sense of masculinity, rather heightens his hesitancy. He has a slight stammer, from being bullied in childhood. When he impersonates Maurice, he is similar, but a younger version of himself, an academic.*

**GEORGE MERRILL/ALEX :** Baritone

*47, stocky, northern, blunt. A moustache. Self-educated but never stupid. Carpenter's lover for twenty years, he has lived with him for fifteen. He runs the household. As Alec he is younger, sexier, idealised, a gamekeeper.*

**EDWARD CARPENTER/NARRATOR :** Bass

*69, very fit and wiry, grey hair and beard. Loose clothing, sandals, broad brimmed hat. Socialist and mystic. Apt to daydream.*

## SETTING

The garden of the Carpenter/Merrill farmhouse at Millthorpe, just outside Sheffield.

The action moves into the novel 'Maurice' as it takes shape in Forster's mind.

The time is September 1913 – an Indian summer.

# INSTRUMENTS

## Flute and piano

# A HELPING HAND

Music – Prelude

*[Slow lighting build to bright 'Indian Summer'. An old deck-chair and a stool to one side.*

*CARPENTER, a hat shading his face, enters carrying a box of peas and a bowl. He potters around, then sits in the deckchair and starts to shuck the peas, using the stool as a table. Slowly, he drifts away into daydreaming.]*

CARPENTER:    Light.
In the evening glow of the sun,
All is light.
Look at those leaves;
A halo surrounds each one.
Look through the leaves
And see the veins.
The leaves become translucent
And alive with light.

Great Krishna,
Lord of life and death;
Shiva the cobra,
His bite will dissolve us all;
Vishnu will evolve us;
Brahma the unfathomable
And infinite god.

Take me, great Life.
When my time comes
Unloose these chains,
Unbind these clogs and fetters.
I will hear the call. I will come.

MERRILL: *[Offstage]* Ted!

*[MERRILL enters.]*

Ted!
I thought you'd be here.

CARPENTER: My favourite place.
The murmur of the stream,
The water so soothing.

MERRILL: Hasn't yer done them peas yet?

CARPENTER: I was thinking.

MERRILL: Daydreaming more like.
Get a move on,
I hasn't got all day,
And a pea risotto
Won't make itsen.
Do I have to do everything?

CARPENTER: Pea risotto?

| | |
|---|---|
| MERRILL: | With turnip tops. |
| CARPENTER: | That's a bit fancy. |
| MERRILL: | I thought I'd do something fancy, With Mr Forster coming. |
| CARPENTER: | Forster! I almost forgot. |
| MERRILL: | Forget yer own name next. |
| CARPENTER: | What time is he coming? |
| MERRILL: | His train were due over an hour ago. Get a move on with them peas – And don't forget young Alec neither. |
| CARPENTER: | Alec Brewster? |
| MERRILL: | Aye. Yer promised that yer'd meet him in t' pub For a game of skittles. He's after you, yer know; Wants to share yer bed. |
| CARPENTER: | Are you jealous? |
| MERRILL: | Me? Jealous? Don't make me laugh! |

CARPENTER:     *[Teasing]* He's a fine upstanding lad…

MERRILL:       But could he make yer tea?
               I think not.

*[He kisses CARPENTER. They freeze. Lights fade on them.]*

*[Lights up on FOSTER (other side of the stage). He is hot and sweaty in an ill-fitting three piece suit and carrying a suitcase.]*

FORSTER:       I hate the country;
               It is so dirty – and noisy;
               All those animals and birds
               Sounding off for all they're worth.
               Trust Carpenter to choose
               Somewhere miles from anywhere.
               Apparently he built his house himself,
               A stage for the drama of his sainthood.

               I must not be uncharitable.
               I'm only tired.
               I have waited so long for this meeting.
               Only fear has held me back –
               Fear of myself, and what I will find
                    there.

*[Full lights. MERRILL and CARPENTER unfreeze. MERRILL goes to greet FORSTER.]*

MERRILL:       Ah, Mr Forster! You found us.

*[MERRILL grabs FORSTER's hand and shakes it rather violently. FORSTER pulls away, disconcerted.]*

FORSTER:　　　　　There were no carriages for hire at
　　　　　　　　　　Dronfield Station.
　　　　　　　　　It was a three mile walk and more,
　　　　　　　　　And of course the locals
　　　　　　　　　Don't know how to give directions.
　　　　　　　　　*[Imitates]* 'Turn right at t' hay barn'
　　　　　　　　　Which hay barn? There are several.

*[CARPENTER climbs angrily out of the deckchair.]*

CARPENTER:　　　*[Irritated]* Don't patronise the people,
　　　　　　　　　Forster.

FORSTER:　　　　　I'm sorry. I said I was tired.

CARPENTER:　　　They are your comrades and the future.
　　　　　　　　　Enough of that,
　　　　　　　　　Give me your hand –
　　　　　　　　　I am glad to see you.

MERRILL:　　　　　Give me yer case.
　　　　　　　　　I'll put it in yer room,
　　　　　　　　　It's all prepared.

FORSTER:　　　　　Thank you – er –
　　　　　　　　　*[He hands his case to MERRILL.]*
　　　　　　　　　It's Merrill, isn't it?

MERRILL:        Call me George. Everybody does.

*[MERRILL takes the bowl of peas from CARPENTER and exits. CARPENTER sits back in the deckchair and pulls the stool forward, beckoning FORSTER to sit.]*

CARPENTER:      And what of you, Mr *Eee Emm* Forster?
                So many with initials –
                EF Benson, GK Chesterton,
                O Henry, JM Barrie
                MR James, RD Blackmoor
                HG Wells.
                All hiding something of themselves,
                Bottled up in initials.

FORSTER:        Come now; Herbert Wells
                Never bottles up anything.
                That is part of his problem.

CARPENTER:      Eee Emm?

FORSTER:        All my family call me Morgan,
                My mother and my aunts.

CARPENTER:      And shall I call you by your matriarchal
                      name?

FORSTER:        It is simplest.
                Mother's in Harrogate for the cure
                Of her rheumatism.

I'd rather she did not know of this visit.

CARPENTER:      Am I that notorious?

FORSTER:        You are well known through your writings.
                They are what made me long to meet
                    you,
                But I held back,
                Afraid of the experience,
                And maybe the emotion.
                I shrink from contact.

*[CARPENTER clears his throat and abruptly changes the subject.]*

CARPENTER:      What is your feeling on nudity?
                Most days I swim naked in the stream,
                I find it clears the mind and body.

FORSTER:        I have never been a great one
                For physical exercise.

CARPENTER:      I can see that. What size are your feet?

FORSTER:        I am size seven. Why?

CARPENTER:      I'd like to make you a pair of sandals.
                Here!

*[He beckons FORSTER to him, that FORSTER should put his
foot in his lap. FORSTER hesitates, then does it reluctantly.*

*CARPENTER removes FORSTER's shoe; measures, then massages his foot.]*

CARPENTER:      You see. So many of your chakras are
                    blocked.
                There is no energy in your feet,
                They cannot connect with the good
                    earth,
                And so you have no roots.

*[FORSTER gives an enormous yawn.]*

FORSTER:         I'm sorry...

CARPENTER:      No, it is healthy. You are opening yourself
                As the flower opens to the sun.
                It is Vishnu working through you.

FORSTER:         Ah yes, Vishnu. I was in India last year.
                I learnt to meditate in Aligarh.
                Troubles always drag on my coat tails,
                Unless I can meditate on love.
                Love is the only thing can keep thought
                    out.
                I love Krishna,
                I meditate on Krishna.
                I don't know if he is a God,
                But I love Love and Beauty and
                    Wisdom,
                And I find them in his history.

CARPENTER:       I have written much on love,
                 On homogenic love,
                 The love of comrades.
                 Are you cut from the same cloth?
                 Do you have a special friend?

FORSTER:         *[Stuttering slightly]* I – I – I do not like
                     to say.
                 M-mother would not like it.

CARPENTER:       Beethoven would have written nothing
                 If he wrote to please his mother.
                 Look at the arietta of his last sonata;
                 Like the unfolding of a child's face,
                 Like the carol of a lark,
                 Like the sunlight on the sea.
                 You can be sure Maria von Beethoven
                 Would neither understand it
                 Nor like it.
                 Perhaps I shall play it for you
                 After dinner.

MORGAN:          *[Shyly at first]* I play piano too,
                 Perhaps we can duet... *[Becoming more
                     excited]*
                 What do you think?
                 The Grosse Fugue, maybe...

CARPENTER:       But would you give it passion?
                 Technique is nothing without feeling.

Oh Morgan, all this inhibition
Will be the death of you,
The death of your soul.
It is already destroying you as an artist.

FORSTER:       How do you know that?

CARPENTER:     You have written nothing for three
               years.
               Before then you ploughed old furrows,
               Because you will not feel.

FORSTER:       I cannot –

CARPENTER:     Cannot? Not even to yourself?

*[A long pause. FORSTER stands, nervously.]*

CARPENTER:     Yes…?

FORSTER:       *[Timidly]* I am an unspeakable of the
               Oscar Wilde sort.

CARPENTER:     Again. Louder.

FORSTER:       I am an unspeakable of the Oscar
               Wilde sort.

CARPENTER:     Wilde. What a dreadful influence!
               I could publish nothing then.

He set the cause of homogenic love
Back a generation, maybe longer.
A shallow, stupid man;
There was no comradeship in him.

FORSTER: I was fifteen when he was put to trial,
A boy at Tunbridge School,
Much despised for hating games
And being effeminate.
I became as quiet as I could,
Not to attract attention,
While I dreamt of my ideal friend.

*[MERRILL re-enters.]*

MERRILL: Right, the peas are set to cook,
The rice to boil.

FORSTER: You work so hard, George.

MERRILL: I has to, I'm a servant.
*[Indicating CARPENTER]* He pays the
 servant tax for me –
Fifteen bob a year! –
So I must earn my keep.

CARPENTER: Come now, George, you know
It's just for form's sake,
To stop the wagging tongues.

| | |
|---|---|
| MERRILL: | Who does he think he's fooling?<br>*[To CARPENTER:]* Everybody knows,<br>   love – and why not? |
| FORSTER: | The words are so unpleasant:<br>Sodomite, catamite, pederast –<br>Even the better words are not quite<br>   nice:<br>Mary Jane, Uranian. |
| MERRILL: | I just call it pleasant.<br>A labour of love… |
| FORSTER: | A love you do not hide at all. |
| MERRILL: | Why should I? It suits me fine. |
| FORSTER: | I wish I had a friend like you,<br>Someone to stand by me,<br>To go through life together. |
| MERRILL: | Yer will have, Morgan.<br>Trust in me,<br>Trust in yersen.<br>Believe you are worthy to receive love |

*[He puts his hand on FORSTER's back and pats it. His pat turns into a gentle stroke, and he works his hand down FORSTER's back, onto the top of his buttocks. This becomes slow-motion, unreal. FORSTER turns towards the front of the stage to address*

*the audience – spoken – while the music describes the internal process FORSTER is going through.]*

FORSTER:    *[Spoken]* George Merrill made a profound impression on me. He touched my backside, gently and just above the buttocks. Nothing suggestive, but still subversive. I believe he touched most people.

CARPENTER:    He was like a cat,
Always rubbing up against all and sundry.

FORSTER:    The sensation was unusual, and I still remember it, as I remember the position of a long-vanished tooth. It was as if he were taking ownership of me. No, not of me, exactly, but of my psyche, and my fear.

MERRILL:    This is what it feels like
To have a lover.

FORSTER:    I felt the heat of it,
The playfulness.

CARPENTER:    It was Krishna playing,
As he played with the milkmaids
And stole their clothes

While they were bathing.

MERRILL:               Whoever heard of Jesus playing?
Jesus never played, and
That's why I can't take a Christian God.

MERRILL/CARPENTER:    Krishna must destroy,
To build you up and make
you new.

FORSTER:             *[Spoken]* It was as much psychological
as physical. It seemed to go straight
through the small of my back, into
my ideas, without involving my
thoughts. If it really did this, it was
an example of Yogic mystic thought,
the like of which Carpenter
believed; it showed that this was that
exact moment when I conceived. I
was determined that in fiction
anyway two men should fall in love
and remain in it, for the eternity
that fiction allows.

CARPENTER:         The wall between subject, object,
Falls away with higher consciousness.
It touches, hears, sees, is
All that it perceives,
Without motion, change or effort,
But with the vast unprecedented joy

To cosmic and universal parts of man.

MERRILL/CARPENTER:     Tell us a story, Forster.
                       Tell us a story, Morgan.

CARPENTER:     Full of light –

MERRILL:       Full of hope –

BOTH:          Full of love and rapture –

MERRILL:       It has to have a happy ending.

CARPENTER:     Yes, it has to have a happy ending.

FORSTER:       A happy ending is imperative.

*[FORSTER puts his arms around MERRILL. They become MAURICE and ALEC (from his novel 'Maurice'). CARPENTER becomes the NARRATOR.]*

*[A church clock chimes four. MAURICE and ALEC fall asleep as the NARRATOR comes forward to address the audience.]*

NARRATOR:      They slept apart at first,
               As if it worried them, being near.
               Towards the morning they began
               To creep so gently to each other,
               And woke so deeply in each other's
                   arms.

ALEC:          Sir, the church has gone past four.

MAURICE:       Not sir, I am Maurice. Maurice…

ALEC:          But the church has –

MAURICE:       Damn the church.
               Did you ever dream
               Of some fine, strong, imperishable
                   friend,
               Someone who will last your whole life
                   through,
               And you through his life too?
               I suppose it cannot happen outside
                   sleep,
               If truth be told.

ALEC/NARR:     A happy ending is imperative.

ALEC:          I do so long to talk with my arms
                   around you,
               And share with you everything.
               It now seems sweeter to me
               Than words can say.

NARRATOR:      Alec snuggled closer,
               More awake than he pretended,
               Warm, sinewy, happy;
               Happiness enfolded Maurice too.

MAURICE:     Time to get up, boy. Morning.

ALEC:     You get up then.

MAURICE:     How can I move, the way you're
                     holding me?

ALEC:     Aren't yer the fidget?
                     I'll teach yer to fidget.

*[He kisses MAURICE.]*

                     You alright, love? You comfy there?
                     Rest your head against me there,
                     The way you like it – that's it, more.
                     And don't you worry,
                     You're with me, don't worry.

NARRATOR:     A happy ending is imperative.

MAURICE:     I'll work. I'll get work with you.

ALEC:     What work?

MAURICE:     We'll find out.

ALEC:     Find out and starve out,
                     Ruin of us both.

NARRATOR:     Happy ending.

MAURICE:      I don't care.
I'll see anyone, face anything.
It's a start of getting free.

NARRATOR:      Maurice knew what the call was,
And what his answer was.
They must live outside the law,
Outside class, or family or money.
They must move to France or Italy,
Where men unite, and do not go to
    prison.
For England never will accept
The twists and turns of human nature.

ALL:      It has to have a happy ending.

NARRATOR:      Maurice had confirmed his spirit
In its perversion, cut himself away
From all the ruck of normal social man.

MAURICE:      We must work –

ALEC:      Yes, work –

BOTH:      And stick together hand in hand till
    death.

NARRATOR:      Happy ending.

MAURICE:      The timorous millions own their stuffy

boxes,
But never their own souls.

BOTH:     But we will own the earth, the sky,
Each other.

ALEC:     And now we shan't be parted ever –

MAURICE:     Never, and that's the end of it –

ALEC:     The end of it –

NARRATOR:     There has to be a happy ending –

ALL:     Happy ending
    Happy ending
    *[Fades]*    Happy ending.

BLACKOUT

THE END

# A GAY CENTURY: 4

### 1918: Front

Above Left: *Siegfried Sassoon by Charles Beresford 1917*
Above Right: *Noël Coward in his teens*
Below: *Robert Ross 1911*

# Introduction

*Front* was the second in order of writing of the chamber operas Robert and I worked on, and at that time we still had no conception of a cycle covering the 20th century. Having written *Fishing* and realised it was only 45 minutes long, it seemed logical that it should become half of a double bill, to make up a complete evening. It also seemed logical that the choice of subject was the other gay 'bookend' of Wilde's life, his first love and truest friend, Robert Ross. Ross probably seduced Wilde around 1886, when he was seventeen and Wilde 32; he is credited with bringing him to a realisation of his true nature. Ross himself, Canadian, had come out to his parents, and was content to be a practising homosexual with all its attendant dangers, by the time of the passage of the notorious Labouchère amendment in 1885; he was sixteen.

Though the sexual element of their relationship faded soon – Robbie preferred butch youths his own age to the pasty, flabby Wilde – he remained a constant and wise friend till Wilde's death in 1900, when he became his literary executor. He was never prosecuted for any homosexual acts, though his secretary Christopher Millard was imprisoned twice, and Scotland Yard detectives constantly followed him. He stood by Millard, as he had stood by Oscar very publicly at his bankruptcy hearing – a story re-enacted in the opera. Ross was perhaps the second most notorious homosexual in London after Alfred Douglas. Unlike Douglas he stuck by his devotion to Wilde, rehabilitated him as a writer with a

Complete Edition of his works, and earned enough royalties for the Wilde estate to move Wilde's remains in style to Père Lachaise cemetery in Paris. There they remain in the most famous grave among the famous graves.

In the Great War Ross was a pacifist, which required a great deal of courage, an admirer of German culture who visited German prisoners of war in their camps, a supporter of women's suffrage and of birth control; all of which he undertook with great style and in fading health.

One story to illustrate his particular charm: in 1915 London experienced its first air raids, as bombs which were dropped from Zeppelins came raining down on the capital. Though the physical effect was small, the psychological impact was enormous. After one such raid, Robbie, who lived in Half Moon Street, Piccadilly, discovered an old woman paralysed with fright cowering in a corner of the Ritz hotel frontage, unable to move. Solemnly he offered her his arm to cross the street, and as she stood up, he opened his umbrella on this fine night, as a protection against the bombs. Thus reassured, she crossed Piccadilly safely.

The plot of *Front* springs from an entry in Siegfried Sassoon's diary quoted in *Siegfried's Journey*. Ross found a new role in later life as a mentor to young poets, including Sassoon (with whom he had an affair), Wilfred Owen (whose homosexuality is central to his work, and little acknowledged even today), and Robert Graves. Ross introduced them to important literary figures, arranged introductions to publishers, and helped their work through the printer's.

On this day, October 4th 1918, Sassoon had had a vile day. After being lectured by Winston Churchill on the wonders of war, he was forced to listen to the din of the Russian Ballet – not a pleasant experience for someone with PTSD. He was settling into a quiet companionable evening at Half Moon Street, when they were gate-crashed by two screaming young queens – among Robbie's other wartime achievements he provided a well-known safe haven for men who were 'musical' [as gay men were called] and in need of support, advice or encouragement. These two ruined the atmosphere, gave Sassoon a splitting headache, and broke up the party. Sassoon sensed something wrong as he said goodbye to Robbie. Ross died of heart failure the next morning.

The two insensitive interlopers were Scott Moncrieff, translator of Proust, and the Boy Actor and sometime teenage prostitute, Noël Coward. The whole incident is a name-dropper's paradise.

I have stuck strictly to the known facts save in two respects. Moncrieff is replaced by Coward's close friend and early writing partner, Esmé Wynne. This is to get a female voice into the ensemble, and to mirror the resources used in *Fishing*. The original intention was to be able to double all parts. It also avoided issues of alpha male competition between Sassoon and Moncrieff, which would have diluted the focus of the piece. The other change is to introduce an anachronism, Eric Satie's ballet *Parade*, which was not premièred in London until 1919. However. it seemed just the thing to unsettle the nerve of a shell-shocked infantry Captain, with its score incorporating sirens and pistol shots.

The title *Front* has multiple meanings. It is literally the Western Front to which Sassoon is about to return, despite the best efforts of his friends. It is the interstices between Ross the man and his battles for civilisation and his beliefs. It is the brave Front, the façade which Coward and Ross and all homosexuals had to put on in order to negotiate a life for themselves in these times; a Front which also hides the doubts, uncertainties and guilts which we all carry around. This inner life is revealed in the four interior monologues which are musically interwoven in the last pages, culminating in a resolve to be the best that we can be.

Sources:   *Siegfried's Journey 1916–1920* by Siegfried Sassoon [Faber 1945]
*Noël Coward* by Philip Hoare [Sinclair-Stephenson 1995]
*Robbie Ross: Oscar Wilde's True Love* by Jonathan Fryer [Constable 2000]

# CAST

**ROBERT ROSS :** Baritone
*49, plump, bald. A smoking jacket and cap. A heavy smoker.*

**SIEGFRIED SASSOON (& POLICEMAN) :** Tenor
*32, tall, handsome, smart in his 1st World War Officer's army uniform.*

**PODGE (NOËL COWARD) :** Counter-Tenor
*18, Gangling and thin. Precocious. Open fur coat, silk scarf over a fair-isle sweater, shirt, cravat, slacks.*

**SPLODGE (ESMÉ WYNNE) :** Mezzo-Soprano
*20, Glamourous, slightly eccentric. 3/4 length heavy belted flowery dress, court shoes or buttoned boots.*

**POLICEMAN :** Tenor, can double with Sassoon.

# SETTING

*The action takes place on the evening of October 4th, 1918, in Robert Ross's suite of rooms at 40 Half Moon Street, off Piccadilly, London. It is the night before his death.*

*The main focus is a comfortable, though not sprawling, armchair with an art nouveau covering. At its side an ashtray is on a small table, which also holds a bottle of brandy, glasses, a plate of macaroons and some Turkish delight. A bookshelf is at the rear.*

# INSTRUMENTS

Flute, 'Cello, Piano

FRONT

*[Gradual lights to Twilight. ROSS is in his chair, staring into the fire, a cigarette in hand. He looks exhausted.]*

ROSS:          Tired –
So tired –
So many trials and libel cases
Have worn me out.
I have been on trial
All of my life.

First Oscar was on trial –
Well, Queensberry was on trial –
For libel.
He wrote on his calling card,
'For Oscar Wilde, posing somdomite'.

He couldn't even spell the word,
Yet he was right –
Oscar was always posing.
He might as well have been on trial,
Not Queensberry.
Then Oscar *was* on trial. Twice.
And I and all our kind on trial with him.

*[ROSS goes into a dream of memory.]*

I was with him when he died,
Held his hand on his deathbed

While he was baptised;
Buried him in Bagneux,
Where Bosie stole attention
With grotesque displays of grief –
He who had consigned him there
Through his rash vanity.

History repeats.
When Wilde was gone,
Bosie hounded me through literary London,
Slandered me about affairs with waiters,
Set detectives on me,
Fingered me to Scotland Yard
For going with a rent boy.
I had to sue. I lost.

I should have known from Oscar –
Those of our kind are always in the wrong.

My secretary's in prison now a second time,
My reputation tattered,
The policeman at my door.

*[Lights brighten slightly, Policeman appears at his side.]*

POLICEMAN:    We have information that
You are an art critic,
A pacifist,
A consorter with the conchies,
A sympathiser with German prisoners –

[*Sneering*] You *visit* them! –
A man of feminine and perverted tastes,
And a professed and militant atheist.

ROSS:      Absolutely true.
And I can show you
Documentary evidence to prove it.
So what are you going to do?

[*POLICEMAN shrugs and goes away, at a loss. Lights dim as before.*]

ROSS:      I am not afraid in these twisted times,
But everyone must be careful.

I have been on trial all my life.
Win or lose,
Every trial's a little death,
A waning of vitality,
Till now, when death itself
Cannot be far away.

[*Pause.*]

Or maybe I am dead already.

[*Lights brighten significantly. SASSOON bursts in.*]

SASSOON:   I can't stand it anymore –
These armchair fighters,

With their wall charts,
And pig-ignorant opinions.
They send men like me
To do their killing for them.
Second-hand blood lust,
Murder by proxy.

*[ROSS picks up the brandy bottle from the side table.]*

ROSS:      *[Totally calm]* Have a brandy –
           My last bottle from before the war.

*[He pours a drink into a glass, lifts the glass and sniffs it before passing it to SASSOON.]*

           It's rather good.
           There's Turkish delight
           And macaroons –
           I know your sweet tooth.
           Help yourself, my dear –
           I'm too tired to get up.

SASSOON:   Do you know who I saw this morning?
           Churchill. At the Ministry of Munitions.
           Chips Channon thought
           He might have a job for me
           To keep me from the Front.
           You know what the old brute said to me?

*[He does an imitation.]*

'War is the finest pursuit of man.
It brings out his noblest qualities,
His courage and his sacrifice,
Total comradeship,
Total dedication,
All focussed on one glorious goal.'

*[SASSOON finishes off his brandy and puts the glass down.]*

SASSOON:    And I looked at him and thought,
            'This is the man who killed my brother
               Michael.'
            He sent him to Gallipoli.

ROSS:       At least he spoke from experience.

SASSOON:    Behind the Front.

ROSS:       He was at the Front.

SASSOON:    He only went to the Front
            For the photographs.
            What does he know
            Of guts exploding in your face?
            Best friend blasted to a thousand bits
            Beyond all hope of burial?
            I told him he could shove his job.

ROSS:       You don't have to go back, you know.
            Wounded twice, you've done enough.

SASSOON:    And then, you know what?
            I had to go and see the Russian Ballet
            At the Coliseum. Maynard Keynes insisted,
            Crazy for the dance.

ROSS:       Or at least the dancers.
            Always a ballerina on each arm.
            Maynard without a dancer
            Would be like Charlie Chaplin
            Without his stick.

*[SASSOON laughs.]*

            What did you see?

SASSOON:    'Parade' – or should that be 'Parard'?
            It's by a Frog called Satie,
            And so ugly… *[He shudders.]*
            Dancers going round in cardboard boxes –
            They could hardly move, let alone dance.

            And what a noise,
            What a noise!

            Typewriters and foghorns,
            Smashing milk bottles…
            But when they came to pistols –

*[Two pistol shots. Sassoon ducks, then shudders. He slowly recovers his dignity.]*

SASSOON:    The Ballets Russes has no idea,
            No-one in this country has any idea –
            'Parade' is only twenty minutes long,
            But quite long enough
            To give me a splitting headache.

ROSS:       Calm down.
            Sit here.

[He indicates between his legs. SASSOON sits, ROSS massages his temples. There has been great physical intimacy in the past between them.]

ROSS:       Let's talk of something much more
                gratifying.
            How is the book received?

SASSOON:    It's not selling badly. For poetry.
            It seems to appeal
            To those now against the war.

ROSS:       And they're growing daily, thank the Lord.
            Haig and Lloyd George
            Cannot – *cannot* – draw out
            This blood sacrifice much longer.

SASSOON:    You've always been consistent, Robbie,
            Opposed the war
            When all the world was caught up in
                hysteria.

ROSS:          I had my share of white feathers.

SASSOON:       Another cross to bear among so many.

ROSS:          Hush, dear boy. No more of that.
               Let us savour the peace and silence
               Of Piccadilly at dusk.

*[A companionable pause. A doorbell interrupts. They come out of their reverie, SASSOON stands and goes to the door.]*

SASSOON:       I'll get it.

*[The lights crossfade to reveal, at the side of the stage, PODGE and his best friend, SPLODGE. They are outside the door in the middle of a furious argument.]*

SPLODGE:       No Podge, it won't do –

PODGE:         Why not? I've written you a part.

SPLODGE:       A wretched part.
               A silly dim girl
               Who follows you around
               And giggles. *[She giggles girlishly in imitation.]*
               All the other characters
               Say she's awful, like her mother.

               I don't *mind* being awful –
               In fact, I'd rather *like* to be awful.

|          | But there's nothing to be awful *with*. *[She sulks.]* |
|          | Even her name is dull. |
|          | 'Faith Crombie'. What a bore! |

PODGE:      *[Bristling]* What's wrong with it?

SPLODGE:    Can't I have a funny name at least?
            I know – 'Faith Crumble'!

PODGE:      Faith Crumble?!
            And her siblings I suppose –
            Apple and Apricot –

SPLODGE:    Not forgetting little Rhubarb –

PODGE:      Dear little Rhubarb –

SPLODGE:    An acerbic tot.

*[They both laugh. The tension is dissolved.]*

SPLODGE:    Don't you see?
            We can make lots of crumbly jokes,
            Especially about my mother.

PODGE:      We? *[Angrily]* I will do no such thing.

SPLODGE:    Oh Podge, why can't we write together
            again?

PODGE:        Because this is my career –

SPLODGE:      That much is obvious.
              The part you've written for yourself
              Is not so much a character
              As a walking self-advertisement.

              Charming, talented, handsome, witty,
                  musical –

PODGE:        And so I am.

SPLODGE:      I am too. Well, not handsome, but –

PODGE:        I need it more then you.
              You don't need a career.
              *[Accusing]* You got married.

*[She is deeply hurt by the last comment. PODGE stares at SPLODGE icily. After a short pause he turns abruptly and rings the doorbell.]*

*[The lighting intensifies back to the main set.]*

SASSOON:      *[Irritated]* I'm coming.

*[He opens the door. PODGE and SPLODGE burst into the room, a whirlwind. PODGE eyes SASSOON appreciatively.]*

PODGE:        *[Coyly/camp]* Hel-lo.

*[SASSOON is clearly uncomfortable. PODGE addresses ROSS while still admiring SASSOON.]*

> I hope you don't mind us dropping by.
> Moncrieff said you kept an open house
> For people who are musical.
> I am very musical,
> And talented in many other ways,
> As well as having a divine figure.

*[He sees the macaroons and takes one to eat.]*

SPLODGE:     And so modest with it too, Podge.

PODGE:       *[To SASSOON:]* My nickname.

> I was a podgy youth, and ugly too.
> The sort of child
> Only a mother or a pederast could love.
> I made myself beautiful by sheer willpower.
>
> They call me the Boy Actor.
> I like smoking, drinking,
> And moderate sexual intercourse.
>
> This is Splodge –
> Her function is to laugh at my bons mots.

SPLODGE:     And stop you making a fool of yourself –
             Which you are doing now.

Won't you introduce us? *[Indicating SASSOON]*

PODGE: I'm so sorry. Miss Esmé Wynne –
Actress, writer and chum.

SASSOON: Siegfried Sassoon.

PODGE: Sassoon! My God, what an ass I've been!
Your picture's everywhere!
I so admire your poems.
I read them in the nude
On a rock in Padstow.
You have the most marvellous clarity.
One day I will write as well as you.

SPLODGE: He will too. Our songs are marvellous.

PODGE: My songs –

*[PODGE glares at SPLODGE, then turns his attention back to SASSOON.]*

SASSOON: I sincerely hope so.

PODGE: Do you have your poems here?
I would dearly love a signed copy.

*[ROSS indicates the bookshelf.]*

ROSS:        There are some copies over here.

PODGE:       Thank you.

*[He takes one and gives a pen to SASSOON.]*

             Put 'To Noël Coward'.

*[SASSOON signs, gives the book and pen back to PODGE. He
shows signs of a blinding headache.]*

ROSS:        Sit down, Siegfried.

*[SASSOON sits on the arm of the chair. PODGE pockets the
pen, opens the book and quotes from 'Dreamers':]*

PODGE:       I see them in foul dug-outs, gnawed by rats
             And in the ruined trenches, lashed with
                 rain,
             Dreaming of things they did with balls and
                 bats...

SASSOON:     *[From memory]*
             ... And mocked with hopeless longing to
                 regain...

BOTH:        ... Bank holidays, and picture shows, and
                 spats.
             And going to the office in the train.

PODGE: I hate war, like you.
I was called up, and I loathed it.
The training made me physically ill.
I had to clean latrines –
It gave me a nervous collapse.
Thank God I had a senior officer friend
Who could bail me out.

SASSOON: *[Ironic]* You are indeed fortunate in your
    friends.

PODGE: I have always felt affinity to older men,
Ever since I was small.
When I was first onstage, aged eleven –
I scored a great success as Prince Mussel
In 'The Goldfish' –
I was besieged by besotted vicars.
I allowed them small liberties in taxis
With my inner thigh,
In exchange for a nice cream tea.

SASSOON: You seem to have been living
Entirely for pleasure.

PODGE: When I was fifteen
I was the mascot of the Artists' Rifles.
And now it has come in handy
To get a medical discharge
From the army.

ROSS:          Your hatred, then, of war is second hand.

PODGE:         As, I would hazard, is yours.

*[He realises his faux pas.]*

               I'm so sorry, so very sorry.
               I've been ignoring you.
               I must introduce myself –
               The Boy Actor, at your service.

SPLODGE:       And almost anybody else's.

PODGE:         Hush, child. Hush, child.

SPLODGE:       Anybody at all.

ROSS:          Robbie Ross.

PODGE:         The great collector and art critic?
               I read your reviews in The Morning Post.
               I admire your support
               For the coming generation.

ROSS:          And what are you appearing in?

PODGE:         *[Discomfited]* Nothing.
               I was turned down for *Oh Joy!* by Jerome
                  Kern.

SPLODGE:    But only cos he's too good for the chorus.
            He's going to be in *Scandal* soon.


PODGE:      It's only a small part, but my career will
                grow.
            I have a selfless devotion
            To my own success.


ROSS:       Scandal! The story of my life!
            Always mired in Scandal.


SPLODGE:    *Scandal*, a play by Cosmo Hamilton.


PODGE:      Scandal should stay where it belongs – on
                stage.
            Those who become the stuff of scandal
            Have only themselves to blame.


*[SPLODGE turns on PODGE, followed by SASSOON.]*


SPLODGE:    Oh Podge, don't been so rude.
            So rude, so rude.


SASSOON:    *[To PODGE:]* Robbie, you young slug,
            Has never sought scandal,
            But never hid the truth.

            Nor did he let the fear of it
            Prevent him doing good
            Or showing kindness.

And as for 'second hand' –
Robbie has been at war all his life,
But not in a way that you would under-
     stand.

PODGE:     You mean all that old stuff
           About Oscar Wilde?
           I know all that, it's history now.
           Wilde brought it on himself
           Through vanity and ego.
           He thought he was invincible
           Because he was an artist.

SPLODGE:   What are you saying?
           He was an artist, and a great one.

PODGE:     The artist is the servant of the public,
           Not its master.
           He who lives by the public
           Can also die by the public.
           As for so-called wit –

SPLODGE:   Remember where you are;
           Remember who you're speaking to.

PODGE:     *[On a roll now]* A laboured, shallow, formu-
                laic wit,
           The weapon of a fat and ugly man
           Who knows he is intrinsically dull.
           I'm sure he practised every word he said

In front of mirrors, ere he ventured out.

ROSS:         *[Remembers]* I told him he should flee to
                  France.
                  I told him not to prosecute,
                  But he was blinded by Bosie,
                  That spoilt, vindictive child.

SASSOON:   It was a fine, brave thing Ross did.

PODGE:       There's nothing brave in self-inflicted
                  wounds.

SASSOON:   Brave? What do you know of brave?
                  This man here *[Indicating ROSS]* is braver
                  Than I could ever be,
                  Braver than you can conceive.
                  Think of it, twenty years ago and more.
                  Wilde in Wandsworth Prison,
                  But now declared a bankrupt:
                  The last humiliation.
                  Up again to the High Court of Bankruptcy,
                  Paraded in convict stripes and chains;
                  The public staring, laughing, spitting.
                  Never was man so alone.

                  And this man here, his first and truest love,
                  The morning of the hearing…

*[ROSS rises; they will re-enact the scene.]*

136

...Rose and dressed most carefully:

*[Ross acts out the description of dressing.]*

SASSOON:     Full morning coat, striped trousers,
             Wing collar, cravat, grey spats,
             Tie pin and top hat of silk plush.
             And dressed like this, he came up to town
             To dignify the outcast with respect.

*[SASSOON, moving to the side of the stage, becomes 'WILDE'.*
*He shuffles across the stage as if in heavy irons. ROSS watches*
*intently as 'WILDE' approaches. As 'WILDE' gets near, ROSS*
*steps forward and slowly, solemnly raises his hat. Time seems to*
*stand still. A long look passes between them, in silence. ROSS*
*steps back and gestures politely to 'WILDE' as if to say: 'After*
*you.' 'WILDE' passes on.]*

*[SASSOON reverts to himself. ROSS returns to his armchair.]*

SASSOON:     *You* could not do that.
             I doubt if six men in England
             Could have done that.

SPLODGE:     *[In awe]* You would not think to look at
                 him
             He could be such a hero.

SASSOON:     He did not have to do it,
             Expose himself to shame and ridicule.

PODGE:      My point exactly.
            Only a fool would do so willingly.

[An icy silence]

SASSOON:    You've said enough. You'd better go.

            Coward by name...
            It's men like you who make me glad
            To get back to the Front.

ROSS:       Don't be so harsh on him.
            He has no experience of love,
            And there are many different kinds of
                'front'.
            He will find his in time.

[SPLODGE, realising the tensions in the room, approaches
PODGE and puts a 'sisterly' arm around his shoulders.]

SPLODGE:    We'd better go, Podge.
            Trust you to go upsetting people.

PODGE:      Me?

[PODGE pulls away from SPLODGE.]

            I am charm itself,
            But I cannot abide the cult of Oscar,
            Or the man himself.

SPLODGE: You are jealous.
You're pining for a cult all of your own.

SASSOON: And you are the lesser man for it.
It's why you'll never be so great a writer,
You want too much that people like you.

PODGE: Mr Sassoon – may I call you Siegfried?

SASSOON: You may not –

PODGE: Well, anyway,
It's been enchanting meeting you.
I realise the feeling may be one-sided,
But I keep a book of notables I've met.

*[He reaches into his pocket and pulls out a note-book, which he flicks through.]*

This year alone there's Scott Moncrieff,
Jerome Kern, Beatrice Lillie,
Fay Compton, Bernard Shaw,
*[He flips the pages.]* Oh – and dozens more.
I'll be delighted to add you to their number.

*[He finds a stub of pencil and writes SASSOON's name. SASSOON turns his back on him. PODGE makes the best of it.]*

Mr Ross, thank you so much
For the macaroon.

We'd love to stay, but we have
An urgent appointment
To terrorise Twickenham.

*[He exits flamboyantly.]*

SPLODGE:    Oh, stop it, Podge.

I'm sorry, Mr. Ross, but he can't help it.

*[She follows PODGE out. The lights dim to an evening twilight.
SASSOON is clearly suffering.]*

SASSOON:    This beastly headache,
That awful boy's done it no good at all.
I cannot think for the throbbing –
I'd better go as well.

ROSS:    I'll see you out.

*[He gets up and walks SASSOON to the edge of the stage. They
shake hands, hold the tableau looking at each other.]*

SASSOON:    You don't look well.

ROSS:    I have never been well since I was a child.

SASSOON:    You need rest.

ROSS: How can I rest? I am going to Australia;
A gallery wants advice on buying art,
And they are paying handsomely.
I think I will enjoy Australia.
I always fit in well
With the criminal classes.

SASSOON: Will I see you again before you go?

ROSS: I think not.

SASSOON: What can I say? I owe everything to you.

ROSS: And have given me so much in return.
We have traded well
On the stock exchange of friendship.

SASSOON: I shall be back to the Front soon,
But I will carry you there in my heart.

ROSS: And that, I'm glad to say,
Is as near as I will get to it.
Protect yourself, my dear.
The world still needs you.

SASSOON: And you –

ROSS: No. It has had the best of me.

*[SASSOON leaves abruptly. The lighting dims. ROSS turns into the darkness at the back of the stage.]*

*[Each character, on entrance, stands distant from the rest. They are in the four corners of the stage. Separate spotlights. This mirrors the arrangements for '1935/6: Fishing'.]*

*[Although with the music these four monologues intertwine and overlap, I have written them here as self-standing, so each can be read to show the character's through line of thought.]*

ROSS:          Silence now in Piccadilly…
Just the hissing of the gas,
And the blood beating in my veins.
I hear the pounding of my heart,
Erratic, overloaded.
It feels huge within my chest,
Rising almost to my throat
Until I choke.
Nowadays all I ask
Of the friends that I have left
Is that they last
Until the end of dinner.

I cannot now be sure
That I will last myself.

Soon, soon, my love, my Oscar,
I will join you again.
Not in any soppy superstitious way;

142

I will not follow you into faith.
But I would like my ashes to lie
In Père Lachaise,
Under Epstein's enigmatic Sphinx
With the mutilated genitals.
What a perfect symbol of our lives
And of our fate!

SASSOON:     I will go back again
To mud and shit and flooded dugouts;
To barbed wire, shells,
Machine gun madness.
I see my men,
Scrawny, famished, filthy,
White and shivering
In October rain.
They strip to wash,
Their skin soft and silky –
Not what you'd expect –
And trust in their eyes.
I miss them. I love them.

Damn you, Winston,
You smug belligerent toad!
Why must you be so right?
Nowhere do we feel so much,
Nowhere do we fill our lives so full,
As in this miserable, endless stinking war.
I want to know everything in life –
The best, the worst –

Yet long for numbness, for nothing.

Maybe this time I can take a hit
To end all these confusions.
The lucky ones are out of it,
The dead are well off out of it.

SPLODGE:      Oh Podge, what will I do with you?
A love never to be returned...
I thought one day you might...
Do you really have such – er – affaires?
For all your talk, it's just a front, I'm sure,
To tease the fuddy-duddies.
You are too nice to be
An abomination in the sight of God.

Now I am Esme Tyson-Wynne,
Wife of Flight-Lieutenant
Lyndon Charles Tyson, RFC.
I got engaged to make Podge jealous,
Thought I could make him pop the ques-
    tion too.
Fat chance. I was a fool.
And now my husband flies in Sopwiths
High over the Downs,
And maybe, next week, France.
He wants to lie with me
But I am scared of childbirth.

144

I am too young,
And what I really want's a pal
Like Podge.
Where will it all end?
Can one love two?
The Word of God says No,
So I must fight myself.

PODGE:     No, Mr Ross, you are wrong.
I have known love,
Two years of it before the war.
Two years of constant sunshine
And Cornish idyll...
I was fourteen and he –
Twenty years my senior.
I see him on a crisp white beach,
Sketchbook in hand.
And later in the Foresters,
His brasses gleaming in the sun,
A god in uniform.

And then he died.

'Each man kills the thing he loves',
To quote the mountebank.
And I killed mine
With my tubercular glands.

Always, Philip, always you are with me,
And I will never go through that again.

I will not love, not like that,
I will protect myself,
And not be fooled by truth.
I will hide in plain sight:
'Mad about the boy'
Is better on the stage
And in the mouths of women.

*[The four intertwined monologues become a more formal quartet.]*

ROSS:          There is no fate but I have fought it.

REST:          There is no fate but we will fight it.

ROSS:          I have carved the space to be what I can be.

REST:          We will carve the space to be what we can
                    be.

ALL:           Out of ourselves,
                    Out of our lives,
                    Out of the world,
                    To make our lives the best we can,
                    And finally to make a truce
                    And peace.

### SLOW FADE TO BLACKOUT

### THE END

# A GAY CENTURY: 5

1928: Sauce for the Gander

Above Left: *Compton Mackenzie 1924*
Above Right: *Radclyffe Hall and Wotan at Crufts, 1923*
Below: *William Joynson-Hicks, 1923, when Minister of Health*

# INTRODUCTION

I have had a soft spot for Compton Mackenzie's novel, *Extraordinary Women*, ever since it was republished by the Hogarth Press in 1986. It drew on his experience of living in Capri before 1914, where his wife Faith had an affair with a lesbian Italian pianist, Renata Borgatti, and with an Italian boy, Nini, twenty years her junior. Nini got her pregnant, which necessitated a miscarriage deliberately brought on by violent exercise. When his family forbade him to see her, he lingered out in the street to catch sight of her, caught pneumonia and died.

Mackenzie himself became friends on Capri with the old buggers Somerset Maugham and Norman Douglas, in whose defence Faith spoke when Douglas was tried for picking up boys in the British Museum. As an extremely precocious 15-year-old Mackenzie was introduced to Lord Alfred Douglas, two years before Wilde's death; Douglas gave him a copy of his poems. He also became friends with Robert Ross and Reggie Turner, the two friends of Wilde present at his death. Under their influence he read 'decadent' literature and started parading in purple bow ties and a high double-breasted waistcoat, for which he was expelled from St Paul's School.

When Wilde was found guilty of gross indecency, homosexuality became *de rigeur* at public schools. Mackenzie wrote, 'Bad behaviour became a magnificent fashion; indulgence in it became a mark of intellectual pre-eminence.'

However, he himself remained sexually indifferent. Late in life he expressed his thanks.

'I am grateful to the opportunity I was given to observe homosexuality with a detached curiosity when I was sixteen, because now at eighty I recognise that it is quite possible to play with fire and yet avoid getting burnt.'

*Extraordinary Women* is the work of that amused, semi-detached observer. It is a 'roman à clef', with many friends, eccentrics and lovers from pre-war Capri barely disguised as characters on the island of Sirene. Romaine Brooks, Ethel Smyth and Radclyffe Hall are all there, but the lightly satiric comic touch veiled the frankness (for the time) of the narrative. It is not a satire on lesbians, however, but on an enclosed hot-house society with all its petty spites, intrigues and jealousies. Life is a parade, a harlequinade.

'*The Well of Loneliness*' by contrast is no holiday, shot through with Radclyffe Hall's own masochistic craving for martyrdom. Of course, no movement can choose its martyrs, but Hall, at least in Diana Souhami's splendid biography, comes across as extraordinarily unpleasant. Possessed of a vast fortune at an early age, voraciously seductive yet insistent on fidelity, capricious, egomaniacal, barely literate – dyslexic? – yet convinced she was delivered of a literary masterpiece. She sacked servants at will, had pets put down if they displeased her, yet paraded her humanitarianism. Her autocratic control freakery was perfectly expressed in her dog-breeding (dachshunds and gryphons) – and it suits our operatic purpose perfectly that for many years she had a dachshund called Wotan, who makes an appearance in *Sauce for the Gander*. As for her martyrdom, nobody is truly martyred when cushioned by an income of £40,000 a year[3].

Her heroine Stephen Gordon – or maybe hero, since there are many signs in the novel of gender dysphoria – is a thinly disguised self-portrait, not least in her appalling relationship with her mother, who had tried to abort her; the situation went downhill from there. When *The Well of Loneliness* appeared, it was universally acknowledged to be a brave and sincere attempt at a 'difficult' subject, though equally everyone thought it would benefit if Hall lightened up a bit. Opinion about its literary merit was divided.

It took the *Sunday Express* to provide the kind of publicity money couldn't buy, when the editor, James Douglas (no relation to Lord Alfred), opined in an opinion piece that 'I would rather give a healthy boy or a healthy girl a phial of prussic acid than this novel.' He called on the Home Secretary to ban it, since 'Literature has not yet recovered from the harm done to it by the Oscar Wilde scandal.'

The Home Secretary was Sir William Joynson-Hicks, a puritan figure of fun to the post-war generation and to most MPs, but in reality a corrupt and authoritarian figure who brought his office into disrepute by systematically engineering false arrests. This resulted in the compliant Metropolitan Police being sued for compensation and paying out thousands of pounds. He came down hard on night clubs ['Any lover of the beautiful will die rather than be associated with the Charleston. It is neurotic! It is rotten! It stinks! Phew, open the window!']; his bête noir was a Mrs Meyrick, who

---

[3] Nearly £2 million at 2020 prices.

was arrested five times for running clubs ['The Cecil', 'The 43'...]; each time she came out of prison she merely opened a new one elsewhere under another name. As the popular revue song had it,

'Come all you birds and sing a roundelay
Now Mrs Meyrick's out of Holloway.'

For Jix, as he was known, drinking out of hours was a sin second only to pederasty. His campaign though, with its hints at nameless orgies, only made the drinking holes more popular. Mrs Meyrick made sufficient money as a result to send her sons and daughters to Harrow and Roedean respectively.

In addition to labelling innocent strollers as prostitutes or as soliciting homosexuals, Jix came down on all the arts at the merest whiff of obscenity. DH Lawrence had 13 pictures seized from the Warren Gallery in Mayfair, and only got them back on condition he never exhibited them in England. Jix also seized some works by William Blake. If it wasn't for his prudery, he would bear a startling resemblance to Donald Trump: 'I am not interested in establishing facts by figures. I have been told that Portsmouth is not a sober town, and that is that.' He saw a Civil War in Ireland as a Good Thing, and harassed the UK's 272,000 registered aliens; not for nothing was he known as Mini-Mussolini.

The encounter in this opera is entirely imaginary, but is based in germ on two established facts: (a) that when *The Well of Loneliness* was prosecuted, Radcliffe Hall wasn't, and she was refused permission to testify by the Chief Magistrate trying the book for obscenity, despite all her pleas; (b) Compton Mackenzie was very unhappy that *Extraordinary Women* wasn't prosecuted at the same time as *The Well*. He told the Attorney General, 'You robbed the public of many good laughs. I should have enjoyed cross-examining you.'

Put those two in a room with Joynson-Hicks in a competitive bid for prosecution, add in Wotan the dachshund [dogs are a recurring theme in the cycle] and James Douglas as Jix's own little yappy West Highland Terrier, and you have a work of high comedy with three absurdly self-dramatising characters triangulated against each other in high Verdian drama. Underneath all that, there is a serious question about who is the true subversive – the contrarian who insists that her sexuality must always be oppositional, or the satirist who suggests that the 'pervert' is exactly the same as everyone else, save in the object of her affections.

Sources:  *Compton Mackenzie* by DJ Dooley [Twayne Publishers 1974]
*Compton Mackenzie: A Life* by Andro Linklater [Chatto & Windus 1987]
*My Life and Times: Vol 2* by Compton Mackenzie [Chatto & Windus 1964]
*My Life and Times: Vol 6* by Compton Mackenzie [Chatto & Windus 1967]
*Extraordinary Women* by Compton Mackenzie [Martin Secker 1928]
*Palatable Poison: Critical Perspectives on the Well of Loneliness* ed. Doan and Prosser [Columbia University Press 2001]

*The Well of Loneliness* by Radclyffe Hall [Pegasus Press 1928]

*The Trials of Radclyffe Hall* by Diana Souhami [Quercus 2012]

*The Last Victorians* by Sydney Robinson [Robson Press 2014]

*The Age of Illusion – England during the 1920s and 1930s* by Ronald Blythe [Faber 1983]

# CAST

## SIR WILLIAM JOYNSON-HICKS : Tenor

*63, Home Secretary. Known as Jix, a nickname which is much jollier than he is. He is a relic from the Victorian days, and dresses so – frock coat, wing collar. Non-conformist lay preacher, puritan, obsessed with stamping out pleasure. No doubts, no modesty. Shallow. A joke among his colleagues, known as Mini-Mussolini.*

## RADCLYFFE HALL : Contralto

*48, known as John. Novelist. Author of lesbian novel The Well of Loneliness. Male-identified. Dressed in male suit and tie. Utterly self-confident and self-righteous, but fundamentally selfish, as a result of having huge amounts of money and always getting her own way. Accompanied by a small dachshund, Wotan, a cardboard cut-out on a string. Wotan is a non-singing part, but represented in the orchestra. Doubles with:*

## MRS MEYRICK (Prologue), *a bright, rather camp, not-so-Young Thing – think Sally Bowles, but with an Irish accent.*

## COMPTON MACKENZIE : Bass/baritone

*45. Novelist. Longish hair and beard with upturned moustaches. Wide-brimmed hat and cloak. Very theatrical – has been a touring actor, and his father and grandfather were barnstormers. His sister is the actress Fay Compton (1894–1978). Satiric sense of humour. Lives on Jethou in the Channel Islands. Undermined by bad sciatica. Always on the verge of bankruptcy. Doubles with:*

**STANLEY BALDWIN (Prologue)**, *60. 'Steady as she goes' – exudes calm and complacency – looks like a prosperous pig farmer.*

**JAMES DOUGLAS :** Countertenor
*Homophobic bigot editor of the Sunday Express. Bristly moustaches. A Scot like Mackenzie, but of the dour Wee Free school. Like Jix and Hall, utterly humourless. He is Jix's peppery, yappy West Highland Terrier. Doubles with the* **NEWSBOY** *(Prologue).*

SETTING

The scene is the Home Office in August 1928. A large ministerial desk, with a phone on it, and a pad and pencil.

INSTRUMENTS

Violin, cornet, piano

# SAUCE FOR THE GANDER

Prologue

*[Highly stylised. '1918' in Caption. JOYNSON-HICKS [JIX] is standing for election as MP for Twickenham. He addresses a meeting; the singers of HALL and MACKENZIE are in the audience, as ordinary punters. Fanfare.]*

JIX:              You all know me,
                  I'm William Joynson-Hicks,
                  The hero of the motorist –
                  I back the rights of cars.

AUDIENCE:   Hooray!

JIX:              The war is over –

AUDIENCE:   Hooray!

JIX:              Germany is defeated –

AUDIENCE:   Hooray! Peace at last…

JIX:              Oh, no, my friends, not peace at last –
                  A state of watchful readiness.
                  We must cow the Hun still further,
                  Bomb his village and his town,
                  Bring his German hubris down.
                  We have to punish

Anything Hunnish.

AUDIENCE 1: But that would be to punish
Innocent civilians,
Helpless and unprotected!

JIX: What better time to punish them
Than when they're unprotected?

AUDIENCE: Hoorah!

*[BALDWIN comes forward and congratulates him.]*

BALDWIN: Majority eleven thousand!
Well done! Well done! Well done!
You've crushed the Labour man and won –
Always pays to bash the Hun.

JIX: Time to bash the Hebrew too;
It's time to demonise the Jew.
One moment please –
One other thing I want to do.

*[Turns to audience:]*

And now a word to all you Maccabeans,
Zionists and such like Galileans.
I've lent on your electoral support;
With your sustaining hand I fought,
But now I have no need to be so winning;

I'll climb the greasy pole without you.
This is only the beginning.
So I say, Jews, *[raspberry]* to the lot of you.
I'm heartily glad to be shot of you.


BALDWIN:     What a fine example
             Of our good old British ways!
             Now we can go back
             To the old Victorian days,
             And good old Victorian prejudice.


JIX:         A victory for morality
             And over bestiality.
             What next? What next?


*[BALDWIN turns over calendar to 1919. Enter the Douglas
countertenor as the NEWSBOY. Spoken, or shouted:]*


NEWSBOY:     Extra! Extra!
             Massacre in Amritsar!
             Unarmed crowd – Colonel Dyer –
             Ordered troops to open fire –
             Casualties in hundreds, maybe higher!


*[NEWSBOY exits.]*


JIX:         Quite right too.
             We have to show the Indian we're boss;
             There's English values to put across.
             And, in case you've all forgotten,

We've got to sell him lots of cotton!

BALDWIN:     Oh, well done, Jix! We'll keep the Empire
             yet.
             Would you like to be a baronet?

JIX:         I don't mind if I do.

[Calendar goes to 1923.]

BALDWIN:     And will you join the cabinet?

JIX:         I don't mind if I do.

BALDWIN:     I think I've got a vacancy...
             The Home Office – I think it's free.

JIX:         I'd rather like that too.

BALDWIN:     It's yours.

[Turns calendar to 1924. They shake hands. A tremendous
chord. JIX is revealed in all his power.]

JIX:         I am the Home Secretary!
             I am the ruler of the Kingdom now!

BALDWIN:     [Falling back horrified at the monster he's created:]
             Great heavens!
             I'd rather be back in Worcestershire,

Breeding my Tamworth pigs,
Than try to keep a muzzle on
Sir William Joynson-Hicks!

*[He exits. JIX looks round, self-satisfied.]*

JIX:        *[Melodramatic declaration:]*
Yes, there will be many changes.
I am the master now…

*[Enter JAMES DOUGLAS. Calendar change to 1926.]*

DOUGLAS:      Hail, hail, mini-Mussolini,
Idol of the Wee Free,
We think you're the bee's knees,
And, whatever vice you're trying to sup-
press,
We guarantee support from the Sunday
Express

JIX:        Good boy, good boy. *[He pats DOUGLAS.]*
Now – Fetch!

*[DOUGLAS bounds off.]*

JIX:        Where are the standards?
Where is the respect?
Where is the authority?
Licence is unchecked.

*[DOUGLAS returns, a newspaper in his mouth. JIX takes it.
Excitedly DOUGLAS points at stories, his tail wagging.]*

DOUGLAS:    Sexy dancing everywhere –
                Flappers flapping in the air –
                Charleston – phew! – what a stink!
                Culture trembling on the brink.

JIX:               Frenzied with intoxicating drink
                From which all righteous people shrink.

DOUGLAS:    Close those clubs!
                Arrest those whores!
                They've got to learn
                Respect for laws!

JIX:               Round up the aliens!
                Round up the socialists!

*[JIX is frothing and about to get wildly carried away.
DOUGLAS worries at his sleeve.]*

DOUGLAS:    *[Prompting]*
                Drunks… Drinking on the Sabbath…
                Drinking out of hours…

JIX:               Oh sin, oh shame –
                Almost worse than pederasty!

DOUGLAS:    Sex in the streets… filth!

JIX:              *[Coming back]* Yes... Yes...
                  I will mop up all the sex in London.

*[Enter MRS MEYRICK.]*

MRS MEYRICK:   You'll need a very large bucket, duckie.

JIX:              Who are you, madam?

MRS MEYRICK:   Kate Meyrick. Nightclub owner.
                  'The 43' –

DOUGLAS:       Notorious haunt of artists and of pansies –

MRS MEYRICK:   I want to thank you for your good
                      work,
                  Drumming up my trade.
                  Never was sin made more attractive.
                  'Come to The 43, for orgies every
                      night!'
                  They're flocking in.

JIX:              I closed you down.

MRS MEYRICK:   I know. I just opened up again next
                      door.
                  That's all you're doing, don't you know.
                  Beating the poor pederasts from bar to
                      bar
                  Like pheasant.

165

JIX:              But what about the police?

MRS MEYRICK:      The police are doing very nicely too.
                  The handouts help to supplement their
                      pay –
                  Which, as you know, is not the most
                      generous.


JIX:              You should be in prison.

MRS MEYRICK:      I have been, thank you very much.
                  Five times. A proper education, that it
                      was.


JIX:              You are an immoral woman.

MRS MEYRICK:      No, Sir William, I am a rich woman.
                  I've had seven children,
                  Put four of them through public
                      school,
                  And will the other three.
                  One day they'll marry the nobility.
                  I just want to say, Keep up the good
                      work.
                  Harrow and Roedean don't pay for
                      themselves.
                  Toodle-pip!


*[She goes out singing a snatch of a song from a revue:]*

Now all you birds come sing a round-
    elay,
Now Mrs Meyrick's out of Holloway.

[*DOUGLAS follows her to the door, snapping at her heels. Fade to blackout.*]

Scene One

*[Calendar set to 1928. DOUGLAS reappears with another newspaper in his mouth. Deposits it in front of JIX.]*

JIX:          Ah, the Sunday Express!
             The voice of sanity and cleanliness!

*[DOUGLAS points eagerly to it. JIX reads:]*

JIX:          'The Well of Loneliness
             By Miss Radclyffe Hall...
             Unspeakable horror...
             Utterly degrading...
             Rather give a healthy boy or girl
             A phial of prussic acid
             Than this novel.
             Shade of Oscar Wilde...
             Still polluting our novels and our plays...'

DOUGLAS:      Sexual inversion! Sexual perversion!

JIX :         What's the difference?

DOUGLAS:      Don't know. Don't care. It's all filth!

*[JIX keeps reading. DOUGLAS whips himself into a yapping frenzy.]*

             Flaunting!
             Public places!

Pestilence!
Young lives!
Leprous as dog dirt,
On the streets
Everywhere!

*[He sees it on his shoe and tries to rub it off furiously.]*

On your shoes!
Euch! Euch!
Clean it up!
Clean it up!
Use the law!
Sunday Express demands:
Use the law!

*[RADCLYFFE HALL appears dramatically, a figure of vengeance like Azucena in 'Il Trovatore'. She has a cardboard cut-out dachshund, WOTAN, on wheels which she pulls on a string.]*

HALL:       Yes, yes, use the law!

DOUGLAS:    Use the law!

HALL:       Yes, the law!

BOTH:       We demand the law!

*[DOUGLAS does a double take, this is not what he expected.]*

DOUGLAS: Miss Hall!

HALL: Yes, I am she whom you have so traduced,
Whose name you have so trampled in the
dust.
I will have justice!
I will have retribution!
I will have the law!

JIX: I will be the judge of that.

HALL: Oh, will you? You miserable maggot of
morality,
You mite of mediocrity –
Sit, Wotan!

*[DOUGLAS bares his teeth and growls.]*

DOUGLAS: Spawn of Satan!

JIX: Sit, Douglas!

HALL: I have written *Loneliness* in blood.
Yes! In my heart's blood!
It has taken my heart, my lights,
My liver and my soul.
*[Fierce]* Prosecute me!
Yes, prosecute the poor tormented thou-
sands!
I will stand for all of them;

I will stand in the dock and say,
'Yes, I am an invert!
Do with me what you will!'
I'll plead for the accursed and the afflicted;
We will not be condemned
For that which God has made us!

*[To WOTAN:]* I said sit!

DOUGLAS:     Sucker on the teat of turpitude!

JIX:         *[To DOUGLAS:]* I said sit!

HALL:        You cannot silence me.
             I will have my day in court,
             And I will be heard.

JIX:         Madam, you are immoral!

DOUGLAS:     Madam? Sir?
             Which? Which?
             Monocle!
             Catamite!

HALL:        *[Calm]* Not catamite, not I.
             A catamite is the invert's mate.

DOUGLAS/JIX:   Lady Una Troubridge!

HALL:        Lady Una is no catamite!

You will not besmirch milady's name.

JIX:          You and she – notorious –
              Your filthy practices!
              Headlines in the papers!
              Eight years ago
              'Lesbians' were on the tongue
              Of every woman in London.

DOUGLAS:      Should have banned 'em!

JIX:          Almost did!
              House of Lords wouldn't have it –
              Thought it would give women dangerous
                  ideas –
              And now this – vile obscenity
              Tries to do the same.

HALL:         The truth must not be feared;
              It must be fought for
              With the strong desire for justice.

JIX:          I am the Home Secretary –
              What have I to do with justice?

DOUGLAS:      Unmitigated filth!

HALL:         How can it be filth?
              It costs fifteen shillings,
              To keep it from the hands of chambermaids

And those in search of cheap sensation.

DOUGLAS:     Immoral earnings!
             Literary whore!

HALL:        My thoughts were on higher things –
             You can tell from the plain black binding,
             You philistine!
             But I can bear it.
             The shoulders of the invert must be broad,
             To face the bitter calumny of the world.

JIX:         You will have all the calumny
             Your twisted soul desires
             If I can have my way.

HALL:        Do your worst!
             Prosecute me!

*[A clap of thunder. In silhouette COMPTON MACKENZIE, another ridiculously melodramatic figure, in cloak and broad brimmed hat. It is a bit like the knocking of the Commendatore in the last scene of Don Giovanni.]*

MACKENZIE:     Prosecute me!

HALL/MAC:   Prosecute me!

*[A little canon on this – Me – me – me; it is very competitive.]*

JIX:           Who, sir, are you?


MAC:           Edward Montague Compton Mackenzie,
               OBE, Légion d'Honneur,
               Serbian Order of the White Eagle,
               Greek Order of the Redeemer,
               Master spy, war hero,
               Novelist and historian,
               Founder editor of the Gramophone
                  Magazine,
               Founder too of the National Party of Scot-
                  land,
               President of the Siamese Cat Club.


*[The dog barks.]*


HALL:          Quiet, Wotan!
               *[To audience:]* He does that when you
                  mention cats.


MAC:           Journalist, billiards player,
               Master of the croquet mallet, island owner,
               Follower of West Bromwich Albion –


JIX:           What is – ?


DOUGLAS:       It's a football club, sir.


MAC:           *[To JIX:]* 'West Bromwich Albion' –
               I love it for the name.


174

You know me, James, of course.
I've worked for you down the years.

DOUGLAS: Mackenzie, by golly!

HALL: You worked for – that – thing ?

MAC: A man has to live, John.
It's all very fine for you,
With your enormous trust fund,
Your retinue of servants,
Your regular dividends.
You can afford the luxury
Of writing as and when.
I have massive debts:
I have Jethou to maintain –
An island costs a lot, you know.
I have an independent wife
Who likes to travel.

HALL: How is Faith?
I saw her in Capri
With Romaine Brooks.

MAC: I have to write for Douglas –
Or anyone.
A jobbing hack, that's me.
I write my way out of debt.
Fifteen novels since the war,
Two a year.

I'll be clear by nineteen-thirty.

Seen my latest?

*[He flourishes it under the noses of DOUGLAS and JIX. He is goading them.]*

> *Extraordinary Women!*
> Mmm – smell the scent of Sappho!
> The intermingled perfumes
> Of lesbians in love!

*[He inhales deeply. DOUGLAS and JIX recoil in horror.]*

> So prosecute it!
> I'd love to have the chance
> To cross-examine you in court,
> Show you up
> For the self-righteous humbugs that you are!
> Besides, the public needs a laugh!

HALL:       *[Picking up Mackenzie's novel]*
            A malicious work –
            It dares to treat the invert as a joke!

MAC:        It treats life as a joke;
            That is what a comic novel does.

HALL:       You trample my desires in the dust.

MAC:        Your self-indulgence, rather.
            John, be reasonable.
            You don't need publicity, but I do.
            You can afford to take your time, I can't.
            Look how long your damn book is!
            Five hundred and twelve pages,
            And mine a mere two-forty.
            You can have the extra pages,
            The double length and more,
            Because you have five thousand pounds a
                year
            Of unearned income.

            *[To JIX:]* Prosecute me, I beg you –
            I need the money.
            Why should she get all the glory?
            All the fun?
            All that martyrdom will turn her head
            And make her even more impossible.
            You're making sure her sickly guff
            Will never be forgotten.

HALL:       And quite right too!
            It is a work of genius.

MAC:        It is tedious and absolutely humourless.

HALL:       *[To the dog:]* Kill, Wotan!

*[They both look at the dog, which of course stays still.]*

JIX:            Mr Mackenzie –

MAC:                        Compton, please –

JIX:            Your book is not incitement
                To go in for this practice.

MAC:            You make it sound like macramé
                Or contract bridge.

JIX:            Whereas –

                *[He finds a quote.]*

                'I am not ashamed of it;
                It was the best part of myself –'

*[HALL knows it by heart and joins in softly underneath, so it becomes a duet.]*

JIX/HALL:       'As a man loves a woman,
                That was how I loved.
                I wanted to give all
                I had in me to give.
                It made me feel strong, so strong,
                And gentle.
                It was good, good, good.'

DOUGLAS:        There! Did you hear those 'goods'?
                Three of them! 'Good' three times!

And no shame!

JIX:    'You insulted what to me
        Is natural and sacred'…
        Natural? Sacred?
        You glorify obscene perversion –

HALL:   Inversion –

JIX:    Any version, it's still obscene.

MAC:    The only thing obscene is the idea
        That a woman rolling in money,
        With a country estate,
        Who rides and hunts and treats her servants
            badly,
        Doing whatever she damn well likes,
        Is one of the rejected of the Lord.
        Try telling that to my compatriots
        In the Gorbals' tenemented slums.

DOUGLAS:  She is an instrument of corruption!

JIX:    Where Radclyffe Hall leads, other will
            follow.

MAC:    How can she lead girls astray,
        Giving her heroine such a rotten time?
        Here she describes her kind – listen! –
        'A miserable army despised of the world,

Who must despise themselves
Beyond all hope of salvation,
With those haunted yet tormented
Eyes of the invert.'

HALL:          Magnificent. So powerful.
               Sometimes I can move myself to tears.

*[WOTAN howls.]*

               See, even Wotan is stirred.

MAC:           The dog must be a literary critic.
               *[He reads again.]*
               'There are so many of us
               With no right to love,
               Maimed, hideously maimed and ugly'
               Is that you, John?
               Are you hideously maimed and ugly?

HALL:          I am maimed inside, for lack of love.

MAC:           I think your Una might say otherwise,
               And all the others you seduced.
               In truth, you know exactly who you are
               And what you want,
               And nothing ever stops you getting it.
               You're nothing but a spoilt brat.

HALL:          Do you hear this, Wotan?

MAC:        A middle-aged spoilt brat.

HALL:       Oh, the coarse, the cruel barbs!

*[WOTAN growls, MACKENZIE threatens to kick him. HALL intervenes.]*

HALL:       Strike not the poor defenceless brute.

MAC:        Jix, can't you see? John is on your side.
            It's a warning to young normal girls.
            John, read the last page, if you're so proud
              of it.

HALL:       I do not need to read.

*[Starts softly, builds:]*

> 'Who were they, these strangers
> With the miserable eyes?
> The marred and ghastly faces
> With the glassy melancholy eyes
> Of the invert.
> 'Stephen, speak with your God,
> Ask why he has left us forsaken.'
> Rockets of pain
> All welded in some great consuming agony.
> 'God, rise up,' she gasped,
> 'Rise up and defend us,
> Acknowledge us before the world,

Give us, too, the right to our existence."

DOUGLAS: Right? What right do devils have?

JIX: Zero tolerance, now and always.

MAC: You are made for one another,
You and Hall.
This is utterly conventional.

I, by contrast, have real lesbians.

HALL: What do you know of lesbians?

MAC: My wife's a lesbian.
Romaine Brooks had an affair with her.

HALL: Romaine has affairs with everyone,
With anyone who's anyone.
That doesn't make them lesbian.

MAC: My wife is always generous
With her affections, especially in the Arts.
There was a Roman pianist as well...

HALL: Aren't you jealous?

MAC: What would be the point?
We are still good friends,

And friendship will last longer far than
passion.

HALL:     I'd kill my Una if I found her out.

JIX:      Jealousy cements a marriage.

MAC:      See what I mean?
          Utterly suburban, both you.
          *[To HALL:]* And what of your own adven-
          tures?

HALL:     That's different. I'm an artist.

MAC:      You are a character in my book.
          With Romaine, and Ethel Smyth,
          All your set from Paris and Capri –
          And you are real, and you are funny.

JIX:      Perversion is no laughing matter.

DOUGLAS:  Hear! Hear!

MAC:      You know not how to laugh.
          If you smiled, your faces all would crack.

HALL:     Inverts earn respect, not laughs,
          Through their never-ending misery.

MAC:      My lesbians have no never-ending misery.

Misery is dispelled
By life, love, laughter,
A fine meal, a rare vintage.

I'll show you.

*[He hands HALL a copy of 'Extraordinary Women'.]*

You are Rory –
Bowler hat and monocle –

HALL:        I have never worn a monocle!

MAC:         You train female boxers and breed bulldogs –

HALL:        Dachshunds –

MAC:         Artistic licence –

And here you are,
Deserted by your lover –

HALL:        Deserted? Me? The idea!

MAC:         Deserted on Capri,
Sitting in the debris of the villa
Where both of you were going to live;
And eating a cheese sandwich.

HALL:        What? No proper picnic basket?

MAC:              You watch the turquoise sea
                  Across the bay.
                  You breathe the pine-filled air,
                  And soothe your bruised affections.
                  The sun beats on the rocks,
                  The waves beat on the shore…

                  Now go from there…

HALL:             *[As before, it starts quiet, but grows in confid-*
                        *ence and force:]*

                  The beauty of the view –
                  Pines and sun and sea –
                  Erased all thoughts of land and home.
                  One was not English,
                  One was not in the world.
                  All one had was this eternal present,
                  Suspended here in time.
                  The windless gold of this October day
                  Diffused a richer peace,
                  Deep in the eternal now,
                  Billowed on a muted murmur
                  Of late industrious bees.
                  All are as one now,
                  Roses and lovers.
                  The ache of disappointed love
                  Fades into the distance,
                  Like a boat heading to the far horizon.
                  Love is a folly,

                           185

Resting with the other follies
Of a thousand years.
Here, now, she was complete,
Secure, herself,
Settled on a warm rock
With bread and cheese.
Only one thing did she lack –
A cup of tea!
She ached for tea,
As ordinary women longed for tea
All over England at this very time.
And as for love, she did not give a fig
If it was gone or not.

MAC:     You see? You see?
'As ordinary women longed for tea' –
She shares her thirst with ordinary women.

HALL:    Where's the grand passion?
Where the true and faithful love?

MAC:     You cannot stand the thought that you are
normal.
You need the sting of martyrdom
To sanction your existence.

JIX:      You read that very prettily, Miss Hall.
Nothing to offend at all.

[*To MACKENZIE:*] Not perverse, only –
eccentric…

MAC:  You miss the point completely.
My lesbian with her healthy sanity,
Her truly English sanity,
May lose her love, but yet still need her tea.
This is not a tortured Sapphic,
But a woman who can love,
Yet live with loss of love.
There is nothing strange about her
Or others like her,
But what is forced on them
By Jix and Douglas and their ilk.
They live, they laugh, they love; and when
they love –
'What fools these mortals be.'

HALL:  I am made immortal by my love.

MAC:  Your love in perpetual opposition.

JIX:  A love never to be countenanced!

DOUGLAS:  Outcast!

MAC:  Where is your ease?
Where is your joy in life?

HALL:  I desire no joy, if I have my love.

MAC:        But love is joy,
            And joy the goal of all,
            The right of all.
            And you shall have it…

JIX:        Not while I live!

DOUGLAS:    Nor me!

MAC:        …if you accept that all are similar,
            Men and women,
            Except for the trifling object of their love.

JIX/DOUGLAS:    Never!

HALL:       Never!

MAC:        The three of you agree, then?
            She is monstrous, strange?

HALL:       I shall be strange if I want –
            But I shall be accepted.

MAC:        That is but grudging toleration.
            I am the true revolutionary.
            I draw the woman in every lesbian,
            And the lesbian in every woman.
            I say again –
            Prosecute me!

HALL:      No – me!
           I have the right to martyrdom.


MAC:       Who wants to follow you to misery?
           Follow me to delight.
           Prosecute me – prosecute us both,
           That's only fair!
           What's sauce for the goose…


JIX:       You have not the foul sweet odour
           Of corruption and decay.
           I open up *The Well of Loneliness*
           To the stench of rotting orchids.


HALL:      The smell's the smell of incense.
           My work is religious.


JIX:       Not smell, stench!


DOUGLAS:   Stench of Wilde!


MAC:       Stench? You know nothing.
           You wave a stick
           At demons of your own devising.
           I knew Oscar's chums
           When I was a schoolboy.
           The smell was all geranium and rose,
           Lavender and jasmin,
           *Mouchoir de monsieur* by Guerlin.

*[He inhales deeply.]*

I smell it yet, the scent
Of Oscar's dazzling friends –
Reggie Turner, Robbie Ross
And Bosie.

DOUGLAS: Bosie Douglas – oh the shame
On the name of Douglas!
I blush to share his clan!

MAC: I remember bright lights
And brighter laughter;
Beautiful clothes,
Rich damask waistcoats,
Silken ties with shining diamond pins,
Gold topped canes,
Signet rings,
Sparkling jewels,
With sparkling wit to match.

DOUGLAS: Mackenzie was seduced!

JIX: Such men are always on the prowl
For youth they can corrupt.

MAC: No, not corrupted. Enchanted
By a world beyond my school,
By the possibilities of pleasure.

DOUGLAS:        Debauched!

JIX:            Pleasure, indeed! Whoever heard of such a
                thing?

MAC:            No-one laid a hand on me.
                Robbie said to Reggie,
                'You and I cannot compete with nymphs',
                When I showed that I was not –
                In the parlance of the times – 'so'.
                Bosie thought me serious
                When he took me out to dinner and the
                    halls.
                He listened to my pushy, flashy talk,
                Pompous beyond my sixteen years,
                As if I was important.
                He made me feel I was a man.

                Think of Oscar's circle,
                One word comes to mind,
                Foreign to you both, I'm sure.
                That word is – kindness.

JIX:            Kindness?

DOUGLAS:                Kindness?

HALL:                   Kindness? *[A kind of round]*

DOUGLAS:    You can seduce with kindness…

MAC:        You have a dirty mind.

HALL:       So you will prosecute?
            Prosecute us both?

MAC:        Yes, prosecute. Let's all appear
            At the Theatre of Boulevard Comedy
            Known as the Old Bailey.
            I will play Harlequin
            To John's Columbine,
            And you can be the fools –
            The old man Pantaloon and the Clown.

JIX:        You, Miss Hall, will bring
            The nation's motherhood to barren ruin.
            The meagre population,
            Depleted by the late war
            And the Spanish influenza,
            Never can replenish
            While women worship
            At the shrine of the clitoris *[pron. cli-TOR-is]*.

MAC:        Pantaloon indeed.

DOUGLAS:    But hang on, Jix, a moment…
            Think…

JIX:        I'll make sure you both end up in prison,
            And imitate your idol, Oscar Wilde.

DOUGLAS: Wait! What if they win?

JIX: How can they win, when I have charged
    them?
This sink of sinfulness!
This barrel of baseness!
I say that they are guilty –
And I am never wrong!

DOUGLAS: Jury may not think –
Juries unreliable –

JIX: They will do what the Sunday Express
Tells them they should do.

DOUGLAS: Juries may not read the Sunday Express –
    Lackaday! Lackaday!

JIX: Really?

DOUGLAS: Not everybody does.

JIX: I had no idea.

DOUGLAS: If they read – grrrr – the *Telegraph*?
*The Daily Telegraph* said,
'A work of art finely conceived
And finely written' –

HALL *[To MACKENZIE, smug:]* My book, not yours.

193

JIX:            Are there pansies even at the *Telegraph*?
                What is the world coming to?


DOUGLAS:        She might call witnesses –
                Literary merit –


HALL:           Literary merit? – No, literary magnificence!


DOUGLAS:        All that guff from Freud –


HALL:           'Notable psychological significance' –
                Arnold Bennett.


JIX:            Another long-haired aesthete!


MAC:            Are you mad?
                Bennett writes about the Potteries.
                There are no aesthetes in Stoke-on-Trent.


DOUGLAS:        Can't rely on juries.
                Besides, they'd have to read the book!
                Who knows what they'd say?
                You dare not risk it.


JIX:            There has to be a way…
                Keep the author out of court…
                Oh, where is Mussolini when you need
                    him?


DOUGLAS:        Try the book, but do not try the author.

JIX:            Seize the books, destroy the books!

*[WOTAN growls threateningly.]*

DOUGLAS:    That goes for dogs as well!

*[WOTAN growls again. DOUGLAS's remarks are punctuated by WOTAN's barks, so it's two dogs yapping at each other.]*

DOUGLAS:    Shut up! Quiet!
            Horrid mutt!
            German!
            Disgusting!
            Little legs!
            Stupid faces!

*[Over all this, HALL tries to get a word in:]*

HALL:       As the author – as the author –
            I have the right –

DOUGLAS:    Authors have no rights –
            I eat authors for breakfast!

MAC:        *[Gloomy]* It's true. He does.

JIX:        I – will – destroy – the – books!

*[They try to tear 'The Well of Loneliness' to pieces. The action should exactly mirror Mrs. DALTON's attempted destruction of*

*ALFRED DOUGLAS's poems in 'Fishing'. DOUGLAS grabs an end of the book, they try to tear it between them, but it's pretty tough.]*

DOUGLAS:    Obscene libel –

JIX:    Trial by magistrate –

DOUGLAS:    No jury, just a beak –

JIX:    A magistrate will order the book to be destroyed.

DOUGLAS:    Bye bye!
No more lesbians!
Grrrr…

*[The book will not allow itself to be destroyed.]*

HALL:    You see, I am indestructible!
My work will live for ever.

MAC:    *[Joins in and tries to wrest the book from the other two.]*
Forget that sickly trash, take mine.

*[He offers them 'Extraordinary Women' – they look at it for a moment – DOUGLAS sniffs it – then turn back to worrying 'Well of Loneliness'.]*

MAC:         Oh, come on Jix, have a heart.

JIX:         A frivolous and sniggering book
             Does not deserve the honour of a trial.
             My mind is fixed…

MAC:         No mind more fixed than yours,
             That's true.

DOUGLAS:     Gathers dust – remaindered – pulped,
             And then is quite forgotten.

             Hail Jix! Hail Jix!
             Who drove the Sapphics out of Britain!
             Made our nation clean again,
             Clean as in Victoria's day
             When family was all.

JIX:         No, never can rest.
             Only a battle in the war
             Against the ever rising tide of filth!
             *[A war cry]* Next stop Lady Chatterley!

*[He and DOUGLAS rush out, waving 'The Well of Loneliness'.]*

MAC:         And so I'll stagger on,
             To one more book to write,
             One more cause to fight,
             More adventures
             And more debt.

There's more fun
To be having yet.
What larks, eh, Pip?
What larks!

HALL:     At least you will be free.
          I will have this weight around my neck.
          Never, never will I write again!

MAC:      You're no wilting violet –
          You'll write again, I guarantee that –
          And even worse than you did before!

HALL:     But I have been silenced,
          I have been torn to shreds!

MAC:      And you will play it to the hilt,
          Incorrigible ham that you are.

HALL:     *[Outraged]* Me? A ham?

MAC:      Takes one to know one, m'dear.
          John, I wish you joy
          Of your miserable martyrdom.
          It's not a club I'd want to join.

HALL:     Mine will be the name all lesbians know
          When yours is long forgotten.

MAC:      I fear you tell the truth.

*[DOUGLAS and JIX join in offstage to turn this into a quartet.]*

BOTH:        That's the way that we'll finesse it,
As a book we can suppress it.
And that's how we'll insist
That lesbians don't exist.

HALL:        I have my purpose to fulfil;
I must defy the world.
I'll show the young and scared,
Much can be done if much is dared

MAC:        For life is fun,
Whomever you may love.
Life is fun,
Whatever knocks you back.
Life is fun,
Grab it while it's nigh,
Don't let it pass you by.
Grab the fruit
And suck its juices dry.

## BLACKOUT

# A Gay Century: 6

## 1932/3: The Berlin Boy

Above: *Eldorado Club 1932 "Here it's Okay!"*

# INTRODUCTION

When I came up with the idea of performing the whole cycle of *A Gay Century* on Zoom, as a contribution to lockdown culture and a defence against going stir-crazy, I still had two outstanding uncompleted projects [*A Shot at the Future* and *Two Into One* – both in Volume Two] and one which I hadn't even begun. This one.

I had read extensively around the period of the Weimar republic, but the actual writing took a week, at white hot speed. As a result, questions hang over it. Is it really a play rather than an opera libretto? Does that matter particularly, because plays have been set wholesale before, notably *Salome* and *The Silver Tassie*? Is it out of place in the cycle because it is set abroad rather than in this country? After all, temporary escape from the repression of British law was part of the experience of the well-heeled homosexual throughout the century: Paris before World War One, Berlin in the 1920s/30s, Amsterdam post-war, New York or San Francisco in the 70s. These are questions only time will resolve. In the meantime, I'm pleased to report that Robert has written one of his most powerfully expressive scores.

I approached the idea with some hesitancy, because the Weimar Republic has been mined extensively and there was a great risk of going over tired old ground. It has been covered with a patina of glamour and nostalgia because of its brief duration, and with an in-built poignancy because we know the fate of so many people involved. Isherwood, and the Isherwood-derived *Cabaret*, was the benchmark, and its influence has continued down to the glossy HBOS series *Babylon Berlin* [2017].

I always found Mr. Norris the most interesting character in Isherwood; he dominates *Mr Norris Changes Trains*, a shady dealer whose appeal lies partly in the mystery that surrounds him, his origins and his activities. This is partly because Isherwood was constrained by notions of what was acceptable to a general readership in the 1930s, but also because the likes of Norris would be beyond the ken of his callow narrator. When Isherwood went back to the subject in his autobiography *Christopher and his Kind*, he provided a lot more information about the model for Norris, Gerald Hamilton, and in the process destroyed much of the aura that made Norris so potent.

Reading the memoirs and biographies of Isherwood, WH Auden and Spender, I was struck most forcibly by the recognition that what we are really dealing with is what we now call sex tourism, with all its implications of sexual exploitation of the poor by the rich. Today it could be relocated to Thailand or the Philippines with no difficulty. It was this harder edge that I wanted to restore to the picture.

I also wanted to restore the politics. It exists in Isherwood/*Cabaret*, most obviously in the song *Tomorrow Belongs to Me*, but it's a kind of easy, almost picturesque, frisson. There is little sense that Fascism –or indeed Communism – arises out of the actions and opinions of ordinary people, including the protagonists. It is always something done by Them, Out There.

The truth is that many of the rent boys described by Isherwood were involved, through Magnus Hirschfeld's Institute for Sexual Research, in mainstream politics, and in Communism. Others put their trust in Ernst Rohm, as an openly gay man well known on the Berlin Scene, to protect them from the rampant homophobia, of Himmler in particular, in other parts of the Nazi Party. Do you flee? Do you hide? Do you collaborate? These are the choices for our German characters; we cannot judge them, because we cannot possibly know how we would behave under similar circumstances.

I have kept the name Gerald Hamilton, but I did not read his biography *The Man Who was Norris*. All the incidents and attitudes here are imagined, though I hope in character. There was an additional model I had in mind. When I was starting out as a writer, I was given some advice by the late scriptwriter and comedy godfather, Denis Norden. He told me that, when writing song lyrics, you should always do it to some pre-existent tune, even if only one in your head. You should never tell anyone what that tune was, and when it came out complete with someone else's music, it would be completely different; but at least you would know that it could be done, right from the start. For plays and libretti it can work as well, but you don't need to conceal inspirations so much. The voice of Gerald I kept hearing was Sydney Greenstreet, the Fat Man in *The Maltese Falcon* and so many *noir* films of the 1940s. With music it will become something else, of course. For the moment The Fat Man can hover over Berlin.

One other inspiration – *The Blue Angel*, the early Marlene Dietrich film in which a schoolteacher, Professor Rath, falls desperately for a showgirl, and follows her into showbiz. Humiliation piles on humiliation as he descends into a murderous madness. How ironic, I thought, to reverse the situation, and have a rent boy corrupted by the worldly charms and experience of a punter. The arc of Professor Rath's degradation didn't make sense for a boy, but the idea that a boy would become infatuated with the life and opportunities represented by a sophisticated and rich punter was entirely plausible. It happens all the time, and the outcome can be just as tragic, whether the young man goes with the older, or stays behind.

While I have tried to avoid the Weimar clichés, I have nodded to them in two ways. Firstly, in making Lotte, the lesbian character, a cabaret singer. It is impossible to ignore the role of popular music in Weimar, and the role that lesbians and gay men played in it, even though that role was largely suppressed and ignored for seventy years. Lotte's songs also provide pointers to the themes of the libretto, in a scenario which is inevitably written in a kind of shorthand. Secondly, in the finale I have used an emblem of the rise of Nazism, a Hitler speech, in a way which I used before in an anthology called *Somebody Bin Usin' That Thing* [2000]. It may be a cliché, but by God it's an affecting one which bears repeating.

Sources: *The Weimar Republic* by John Hiden [Longman 1974]

*The Weimar Republic* by Eberhard Kolb [Routledge 1988]

*Weimar Germany: Promise and Tragedy* by Erich D Weitz [Princeton University Press 2009]

*Mr Norris Changes Trains* by Christopher Isherwood [Hogarth Press 1935]

*Christopher and his Kind* by Christopher Isherwood [Farrar, Strauss and Giroux 1976]

# CAST

**GERALD HAMILTON :** Bass-Baritone
*50-ish, dyed hair, unconvincing toupee, fat. A grandiose way of talking. Totally untrustworthy. Think Sydney Greenstreet as The Fat Man in* The Maltese Falcon.

**PAULI GASTERN :** Tenor
*Rent boy. 22 or so, a knobbly face toughened by country hardships, but attractive in an unconventional way. Recent arrival in Berlin from the country. A certain wide-eyed wonder at Berlin. Tries to be tough despite this.*

**LOTTE LANGE :** Mezzo
*Late 20s, very beautiful in a severe way. Intelligent, political, cabaret performer. Takes no nonsense. Knows her way around, cynical, especially about men.*

**Miscellaneous – WAITER, KPD MEMBER, NSDAP MEMBER :** Baritone
*These can all be played by one person, who might elsewhere be part of the 'orchestra'.*

# SETTING

Berlin, winter of 1932 – 33. Open staging. One bench, two chairs to double as park bench, restaurant table, etc.

# INSTRUMENTS

Alto saxophone, piano, double bass

# THE BERLIN BOY

Prologue

*[A Berlin Cabaret, October 1930. LOTTE in evening dress.]*

LOTTE:     <u>The Boys of Berlin</u>

The boys of Berlin, they are charming;
The boys of Berlin, they are kind;
They never will find it alarming,
Whatever you've got on your mind.

Boys of Berlin, totally pliable –
Randy and rampant, that's undeniable.
Maybe they're not entirely reliable,
Still – they're the boys of Berlin.

See them lining the Kurfürstendamm –
Money for sex is money for jam.
Get a sample of what they're exposin' –
Feel through the pockets of their leder-
　　hosen.

The boys of Berlin are in flower,
They offer themselves every day.
Be quick, 'cos they fade by the hour,
And soon they'll be all blown away.

Boys of Berlin, throbbing and thrilling,
Out with the crowds in the Tiergarten
   milling,
Quite inexpensive, wonderfully willing,
Breath-taking boys of Berlin.

Boys of Berlin, their pockets they're filling.
Marvel at what you can get for a shilling;
Others are planning on making a killing –
Say a prayer for the Boys of Berlin,
If you care for the Boys of Berlin.

*[Exits to applause. Lights change.]*

## Scene One

*[Early October 1932. Outside Friedrichstrasse Bahnhof – the international station. Enter GERALD off the train. One battered suitcase. He addresses the audience directly. A big theatrical intake of breath.]*

GERALD:      The smell of Berlin –
There's nothing like it!
Sweat and mascara and spunk.
More than you can imagine,
More than you could take in a lifetime.
Do you know
There are over three hundred bars in Berlin,
Catering to a special clientele…?
Perverts with discernment and discretion –
Well, not all with discretion, if we're honest.
It's glorious to be back
In the queerest city in Europe.
A walk down to the Spree, I think,
And over the Moltke Bridge.
A stroll along the river will be pleasant
This clear crisp day.
There are always young men fishing there –
Though not perhaps for fish.

*[He starts to walk. Lights change. He is by the river. PAULI is lounging against a lamp post. GERALD walks past. They exchange a glance. GERALD returns. Classic cruising routine. GERALD produces a large cigar. Goes to PAULI.]*

GERALD:     Haben sie Feuer?[4]

PAULI:      I think I have some matches in my pocket.
            You speak German very well.

GERALD:     Thank you, thank you.
            I trained as a linguist for the Diplomatic
               Corps.
            I can lie convincingly in eight languages.
            Er – the light?

PAULI:      I seem to have my hands full.

*[He doesn't. They are behind his back.]*

            Do you think you can reach into my
               pocket?
            You can help yourself.

GERALD:     I'm much obliged.

*[He does so. There is a hole in the pocket of PAULI's shorts. His
fingers grope around. He finds PAULI's member, and is highly
gratified.]*

GERALD:     Charming, charming.
            Are you Jewish?

---

[4] There is a question, which language are they speaking? I hope this establishes
   that although the script is in English, they are assumed to be speaking German.

213

PAULI:     That is not a question to ask a German
           In Berlin nowadays.
           As a matter of fact, I am not Jewish.
           I am from Kolberg…
           In the north…
           We have no Jews in Kolberg.

GERALD:    I know it. A spa town.

PAULI:     I was a spa attendant.

GERALD:    Delightful.
           What is your name?

PAULI:     Pauli…

GERALD:    A charming name.
           You look like a Pauli…

PAULI:     *[Flattered]* Do I?

GERALD:    Indeed you do. Boyish, yet dependable.
           I imagine you as an Ideal Friend.

PAULI:     To me, Friendship is sacred.
           And your name is –

GERALD:    You can call me Gerald.

PAULI:     You have an actor –

Sir Gerald du Maurier.
I saw him in a film.
He played a convict, imprisoned in error,
And he escaped.
He was hunted like a dog,
The hand of every man against him.
But the women all were kind to him,
So kind and understanding,
Because he was a gentleman.
I cried when he was caught again.
He reminded me of boys like us,
All the world against us.
Yes, I can see you are a Gerald:
A gentleman, kind, considerate.

GERALD:     I am a gentleman, yes, by background,
            But I do not draw attention to it.

PAULI:      That is so English. I adore the English.

GERALD:     Really? You must tell me all about it.
            Though we would never admit it,
            We do rather like to be adored.
            Do you have somewhere we can go?

PAULI:      What about your hotel?

GERALD:     That would not be – convenient.
            It is quite a refined
            And respectable establishment

PAULI:          Which one?
                I have been in many
                Respectable establishments.

GERALD:         [Evasive] I am well-known there.
                I have many business interests,
                They might be jeopardised.
                Do you have somewhere?
                Some charmingly insalubrious apartment?

PAULI:          Insalubrious?

GERALD:         Unhygienic... Run-down... squalid...
                Somewhere – working class.

PAULI:          [Protesting] We are very clean!

GERALD:         We?

PAULI:          I share a place with several other fellows.
                It is crowded. We cannot afford other.
                And I am not sharing you with them!

[He winks at Gerald.]

                Do not worry. I know a bar.

GERALD:         A bar? That's much more like it.

PAULI:          A simple bar, no affectation,

Just boys looking for work – or love –
And workers looking for boys.

GERALD:     It sounds marvellous!

PAULI:      Here, let me carry your suitcase.

GERALD:     *[Sharp]* No. That stays with me.
            Papers, you know… Important papers…

*[They exit. Slow fade to blackout.]*

## Scene Two

*[Early October 1932.   Noster's Cottage. A table and two chairs. The WAITER is clearing the table, which has an oilcloth on it.   He is tired and grumpy and his apron is none too clean. He hums Lotte's song from the Prologue – it is obviously popular among the local gay boys. He moves two glasses to the side, and wipes the table down with his apron.]*

WAITER:      Yum bi dum bum,
                 Yum bi dum bum,
                 Randy and rampant
                 That's undeniable…
                 Yum bi dum bum,
                 Yum bi dum bum…

*[There is a stubborn stain on the cloth.   He spits on it and rubs it vigorously. To an unseen/unheard customer off stage:]*

          Yes? What? Can't you see I'm busy?
          Wait your turn.

*[He looks up/off stage and sees the customer is important.]*

          I'm sorry, Herr Professor.
          Right away, Herr Professor.

*[He picks up the glasses, turns to the audience:]*

          *[With venom]* I hate this job!

*[GERALD and PAULI enter – the WAITER indicates the free table and exits giving a wink to PAULI.]*

PAULI:        A table – here –

*[He politely stands to make way for GERALD. Sits after he is settled. GERALD accepts this as of right.]*

GERALD:        The Restaurant in the Hut –
                Well, it is a hut. But I don't see much
                    eating.

PAULI:        Here we eat with our eyes.

GERALD:        Ha! Yes… very good, very good.

PAULI:        In English it is Noster's Cottage.

GERALD:        A cottage? Ha! That is more apt.
                It is cozy. A simple curtain over the door,
                Simple benches.
                This is so authentic. No side.

PAULI:        Side?

GERALD:        No pretention.
                Will you have a cigarette?

PAULI:        What are they?

GERALD:     Players.

PAULI:      *[Disappointed]* I only smoke Salem
            Aleikum.

*[He takes one nonetheless.]*

GERALD:     Then Salem Aleikum you shall have –
            Next time.
            Waiter! A scotch and soda!
            And a *large* brandy for my guest.

PAULI:      How did you know that I drink brandy?

GERALD:     You all do. You always do.
            Waiter!
            Now tell me about your early life
            In Kolberg.
            I want to know all about it.

PAULI:      I was born there before the war.

GERALD:     I fought during the war, you know.
            In Ireland, in the uprising.
            Nineteen-sixteen.

PAULI:      I would not fight in any war,
            Except beside the Friend I loved.

GERALD:     There is that, yes.

Let's not get morbid –
Tell me about your youth.

PAULI:   We had a small farm
Just outside Kolberg,
Inland from the sea.
It was very cold in winter,
Cold and damp and windy off the sea.

*[GERALD comes forward and addresses the audience directly, while Pauli continues his story behind.]*

PAULI:   We had a few cows,
But mainly grew potatoes.
There is nothing harder
Than planting and picking potatoes.
And for what? For nothing.
Money was worth nothing.
It grew more worthless by the hour...

In summer I would go to the beach –
There was a long sandy beach –
With my friends in the *Wandervogel*.
We swam naked in the sea –

GERALD:   *[To audience:]* This is how you get the boys,
By remembering their names
And the story of their life.
Of course, they will all go with you
If you pay them.

221

They are anybody's for ten marks –
Twelve shillings and sixpence.
But what they all really want
Is a great passionate Friendship.
If they think you are their Friend
It works out cheaper.
I must be careful with money.
At the moment I am short of funds,
Until I make contact. *[He indicates the suitcase.]*

*[He takes out his wallet, counts carefully.]*

He won't want too many brandies, I hope.

*[He turns back to PAULI at the table, and sits.]*

Do you like opera?

PAULI:       *[Confused]* I don't know.

GERALD:      I can get tickets for the Staatsoper.
             Erich Kleiber – Marriage of Figaro –
             I know you would adore it.

PAULI:       Don't you have to wear evening dress?
             I don't have any clothes…

GERALD:      I will buy you the clothes –
             When I am in funds.

Where is that waiter?
Oh, to hell with him.
Might I have the pleasure of this dance?

*[He takes PAULI's hand and they waltz off as the lights fade, GERALD leading.]*

Scene Three

*[Late October 1932. Another bar – Die Grüner. PAULI and LOTTE sitting. LOTTE is stylishly dressed in a well-tailored three-piece suit.]*

LOTTE:      Why do you have to invite me here?
                I expect the police to come at any moment.

PAULI:      They won't –

LOTTE:      It's always being raided!
                If only all you boys
                Would give up stealing.
                Or pickpocketing.
                Or blackmail…

PAULI:      Have a heart. We have to live.
                We can't all be as talented as you.
                If you don't like it here,
                Why don't you invite me to the Monopole?

LOTTE:      I can't invite you there –
                Too many former lovers I must avoid.
                You have no idea how tedious it is!
                Love should be like that song in *Words and
                    Music* –

PAULI:      I do not know this.

LOTTE:      The new English revue by Noël Coward.
            Gertrude Lawrence brought the records
                with her
            When she came to Berlin after her filming.
            I met her in the Damenklub Pyramide –
            She comes here to shed her inhibitions.


PAULI:      Did you – ?

LOTTE:      A lady never tells – what do you think?

*[She looks very complacent and sings:]*

            Let our affair be a gay thing,
            And when these hours have flown,
            Then, without forgetting
            Happiness that has passed,
            There'll be no regretting
            One that didn't quite last –

PAULI:      Pretty.

LOTTE:      There's one that you would like more –
            *Mad about the Boy.*
            From everything I hear,
            Herr Coward would be mad for you.

PAULI:      No, I am spoken for now.
            I have found my Friend.

LOTTE: Are you crazy? He is fat, he is ugly,
And he never could be trusted.
Besides, he is a Nazi.

PAULI: I don't believe you.

LOTTE: When you introduced us – remember? –
He put his wallet on the table.
I sneaked a look.
There was a party membership card.
How can you trust him? A fascist!

PAULI: He has been good to me.
Anyone who is not a Communist
Is a fascist to you.
The democrats are Social Fascists
According to you.

LOTTE: Well they are.

PAULI: I do not understand politics –
All these labels.

LOTTE: And he doesn't like women.
No, I don't trust him.

PAULI: I do trust him.
He is kind. He listens to me,
He takes me seriously.
His mind is not ugly,

And as for being fat –
There is something of comfort,
Pillowing your head
On a large, smooth, warm belly.
Sinking in the flesh,
His arms around your shoulders –
I feel so safe. Nothing can touch me.

I hear his little trills and gurgles,
It is like his tummy is talking to me.
And then I sleep – and dream...

I dream of going to England
Where every man's a gentleman;
Where I can work – and keep house for
    him,
In a little flat, or cottage.

That is what I dream.

LOTTE:     My God! Claire Waldorff is right when she
        sings,
    'All men are stupid'.
    He will walk away. You will see.

*[Pause]*     I wish mine would walk away,
    They never do.
    Cling, cling, cling!
    'Why can't we be friends?'
    We were never friends,

We were gaping for each other,
And now we're not – end of story!
Lovers can't be friends –
Neither can those casual sexual partners.
But no, they hang on
To every pathetic scrap of memory:
'Do you remember when –'
'You said – you did –'
No – I – don't;
And no – I – won't.
I remember your salt taste on my tongue
Between your thighs,
And that is quite enough.

Is that the time?
I have to get to the Eldorado –
It's the opening night.
Conrad Veidt is performing the ceremony.

PAULI:      I must wait for Gerald.
He has some business to perform.

LOTTE:      Dirty business, I'm sure…

PAULI:      No! He is a businessman:
Import – export –

LOTTE:      Importing what? Exporting what?
What can he carry in that little case?

PAULI:       Papers... licences... letters of credit...
             He is a big man – a genius –
             He has many deals.

LOTTE:       Bah!

*[She leaves. Fade to Blackout.]*

Scene Four

*[Late October 1932. A Street Corner in the Hallesches Tor district. GERALD is waiting under a lamp-post. Shades of Lili Marlene.]*

GERALD:      There is nowhere colder
Than Berlin in November.
The wind whips all the way from Minsk,
Across the Polish plains.

*[He looks at his watch.]*

Where is Thalmann?
Blooming communists are always late!
Look at Lenin, late for his own revolution!

*[Enter an apparatchik of the KPD.]*

You're not Thalmann.

APPARATCHIK:   How do you know?

GERALD:      I read the papers like anyone else.
His face is always in them.
How do I know you are a member of the
KPD?

APPARATCHIK:   *[He takes out a card.]* My party membership. And you?

GERALD:        *[Producing card likewise:]* My party mem-
                   bership.
               I have always supported the Party.
               I was in Moscow in 1922.
               Fine man, Lenin. An inspiration.

*[APPARATCHIK considers a moment, and then grunts and nods.]*

APPARATCHIK:   You have the list?

GERALD:        I do. And you shall have it.

*[APPARATCHIK reaches for it.]*

GERALD:        One moment.
               Herr Thalmann must have mentioned –
               My commission.

APPARATCHIK:   But it is for the good of the party.

GERALD:        I cannot serve the party if I can't eat.
               *[He holds out his hand.]*
               My commission was agreed.
               In dollars.

*[APPARATCHIK reluctantly hands it over. There is an exchange.]*

GERALD         Here.

*[He hands over a list. As he counts the money:]*

> You will thank me. I have saved you.
> If the party had found out
> You meant to chisel them,
> You would likely have ended in the Spree...
>
> It is a list of targets for the Brown Shirts
> And the planned dates of the attacks.
> Jewish... left wing... trade unions... ah,
>    homosexual...

APPARATCHNICK:  Where did you get this?

GERALD:     Ernst Rohm's private office.
           Quite authentic, I assure you.

APPARATCHNICK:  But did no-one see you?

GERALD:     It was a private meeting.
           He was interested in – certain specialist
              magazines
           From America I was able to offer him.
           I offered him a sample to peruse,
           And while he was deep in contemplation...
           On his desk, a carbon copy...

APPARATCHIK:   Thank you.
           Forewarned is fore-armed.

The party will remember this with gratit-
    ude.
Who shall I say – ?

GERALD:          Better leave my name out of it.
                 Say that it came from Pauli –
                 Pauli Gastern.

                 *[To audience:]*
                 It will stand him in good stead
                 If the Commies come to power.
                 You know it makes sense.

                 **BLACKOUT**

Scene Five

[*4th November 1932. The Moka Efti club. LOTTE in performance mode again. She is Diana the Huntress, in classical tunic,
with a bow, and arrows over her shoulder.*]

LOTTE:        I love to swim in the Wellenbad
Where flesh is flaunted by the yard
The girls are easy and the men are hard
Out in the park in the open air.

Forget your clubs and forget your balls;
Forget their lure when it's – 'Nature calls!'
Far from the city and from these four walls
The wind can blow through your wanton
    hair.

There are lots of sights to see –
Do you want to come with me?

I'm going out on a deer hunt –
Got my arrows and my bow.
Some folk think it's a queer hunt,
But what do some folk know?

I'm searching there, I'm searching here,
I'm searching far, I'm searching near,
I won't despair that a deer will appear
And put me in a whirl.
Though I've seen a bear, I'm very clear

I don't want a bear, I want a deer.
I'm searching for a deer,
Searching for a deer,
Searching for a dear, dear girl.

I've got a mind to try a few,
I've got my eye on one or two –
Perhaps I've got my eye on you.
I'm searching for a deer,
Searching for a deer,
Searching for a deer,
Searching for a dear, dear girl.

Through the forest I'll pursue,
But if a deer is not in view,
Perhaps a little pussy will do!
Searching for a dear, dear girl.

*[She acknowledges applause, bows, then holds her hand for silence. Spoken:]*

Seriously, ladies and gentlemen. On Sunday
we have the Reichstag elections. I don't
believe in this rotten Weimar republic, but
the one thing I do know is, we must keep
the Nazis out of power. The only way to
do that is to vote for the KPD, the Communist Party of Deutschland. Remember
a vote for the Communists, a vote for
Ernst Thalmann, is a vote against the

Nazis, against Adolf Hitler, and against the
thugs of Ernst Rohm's Brown Shirts.

*[March]*

Let's drag the Brown shirts down!
Let's drive them off the streets!
We have to kick them out of town,
Kick them in their big brown seats.
We have a duty, we have to fight –
It's no time for being polite.
Fighters for right we are –
Three cheers for the Antifar!

*[She is joined by the APPARATCHIK from the last scene, who
helps to lead the audience in a chorus.]*

Let's turn the Brown shirts red!
Now we must spill their blood!
And when we're sure they've bled,
Trample the swine in the mud!
Shoulder to shoulder, let us advance,
Never give the fascists a chance.
So let's all sing Hurrah!
All hail to the Antifar

*[There is the sound of a brick coming through a window, and
screams as offstage Nazi thugs lay into the audience. LOTTE
makes to go towards the fight to join in. The APPARATCHIK
draws her away.]*

APPARATCHIK:    Now is not the time –
                    The party needs you.

*[He leads her away, protesting. The clamour rises…]*

## BLACKOUT

Scene Six

*[November 8th, 1932. Noster's Bar again. PAULI and GERALD.]*

GERALD:      Waiter! A scotch and a large brandy.

PAULI:       Lotte says you are a Nazi.

GERALD:      I am not.

PAULI:       You joined the party.

GERALD:      I am a member of the RAC
             But I do not drive a car.

             *[A look from PAULI]*
             An organisation for motorists.
             It runs an excellent club restaurant and
                  hotel.

             Look, Pauli. There are some things
             It is better not to know too much about.
             *[Vaguely]* Politics…

PAULI:       Are you a spy?

GERALD:      Shhh!

*[WAITER appears with the drinks. Puts them down. Waits to be paid.]*

GERALD:     Put them on my tab.

WAITER:     No, no more tab.
            You have too much debt.

GERALD:     Pauli... liebchen... I have a difficulty...
            A temporary embarrassment, I assure you.
            Only till I get the bank draft from London.
            Could you be so kind?

*[PAULI hesitates...]*

            Purely temporary!
            I will of course repay you
            When my cash arrives.

*[Still he hesitates...]*

            For friendship's sake...

*[PAULI gets out his money immediately.]*

            If you could settle the whole account...

*[PAULI holds up his wallet. The WAITER extracts some notes. It
is more than PAULI expected, more than he can really afford.]*

GERALD:     Pauli, my angel, you are truly one in a
              million.
            That was the act of a true friend.

*[He puts his arms round PAULI, who settles comfortably into them, his concern forgotten.]*

GERALD:     Tell me about your time in Kolberg.

PAULI:      I've told you everything.

GERALD:     I want to hear it again.
            I like to hear you talk,
            I like the sound of your voice,
            Your rough country voice. *[He kisses PAULI
               gently.]*
            Go on.

PAULI:      Where shall I start?

GERALD:     The steam baths –
            I like to hear about them.
            You were sixteen…

PAULI:      My father had died in the flu
            When I was ten.
            I had to work the fields;
            So did my mother.
            It was back-breaking
            And I was still at school.
            Do you wonder when we went to the beach
            I looked with envy at the fat burgers
            In their striped costumes,
            In their bathing huts,

And on the pleasure boats?

I stood outside the Maximilian Spa Hotel
One day when I was twelve;
The manager came out to me.
I did not know anything then,
But I could tell he liked me.

'You look a likely lad.
Well-set-up. Strong.
Are you willing?
We like boys here 'willing and discreet'.'

GERALD:      Willing and discreet – charming.
It sounds a fine hotel.

PAULI:      It was. I met many gentlemen;
My mother did not have to work again.
Money was worth nothing,
But I took food from the hotel.

One day, a year ago,
A man offered to take me to Berlin.
Berlin! How could I refuse?
He was married, to be sure,
But he set me in a small apartment
In Charlottenburg.
It was so exciting – all the lights!
The crowds – the noise!

Then his wife found out – he said –
And I was on the streets.

GERALD: Ah yes, married men!
You can never trust a married man.

PAULI: I have trusted too often.
They always make promises
They never keep.

GERALD: Your poor bruised heart…
Why didn't you go back to Kolberg?

PAULI: I could not go back –
I did not want to go back –
To the cows – and the potatoes.

GERALD: But your poor mother?

PAULI: She was religious,
I would bring her shame.

GERALD: But she is still your mother.

PAULI: How can she be my mother,
When I am 'no son of hers'?

GERALD: Tell me about the boys again…
The naked boys on the beach…

*[LOTTE enters, excited. She has the remains of a black eye.]*

LOTTE:    The election results have come,
          They are in the evening papers.
          The Nazis have lost thirty seats!
          The tide has turned!
          The KPD has gained eleven!

GERALD:   The Nazis are still the largest party.

LOTTE:    But they are not unstoppable now!
          *We* can stop them.
          The Nazis now will never get to power,
          They have lost their impetus.

PAULI:    *[changing the subject]* How is your poor eye?

LOTTE:    Better.

PAULI:    *[To GERALD:]* She was set on, going home
          From the club on Friday.
          The Nazis broke the club up.

GERALD:   That should not have happened.

LOTTE:    You sound like you know something…

PAULI:    I have talked with Gerald,
          He is not a Nazi.
          It is something special,

Something secret.

GERALD:    Please, Pauli –

LOTTE:     This is *scheiss*.

GERALD:    I really can't discuss it.
           Come, Pauli,
           Let us find somewhere quieter
           And more sympathetic –

*[He gets up to leave. PAULI follows him.]*

LOTTE:     Pauli –

PAULI:     *[A hopeless gesture]* He is my Friend.

LOTTE:     He is not your friend.

*[They leave. She calls out after him.]*

He is not your friend, Pauli.

## BLACKOUT

## Scene Seven

*[9th November, 1932. Unter den Linden, outside the State Opera. NAZI is waiting under the street lamp. He has a swastika armband. Enter GERALD.]*

GERALD:    Ah, Herr Armfeld.
           You can always rely on the fascisti
           To be on time.
           Like Mussolini's trains.

NAZI:      We are not fascisti,
           We are socialists – National Socialists.

GERALD:    Yes, yes. *[Perfunctory]* Heil Hitler!

NAZI:      Do you have it?

GERALD:    The passport? Of course I do.

*[He brings out a passport. Dangles it invitingly. He is playing with the NAZI.]*

NAZI:      *[Impatient, snaps his fingers]* Quickly. Give it
           here.

GERALD:    Why are you in such a hurry?
           The train to Denmark isn't for three hours.

NAZI:      How do you know?

What do you know?

GERALD:    I read the papers.
           A girl who was dancing at the Moka Efti
           Was set on by a gang –
           The paper called them hooligans.
           And now she has died.
           I am assuming one of yours
           Was responsible
           And needs to go away,
           To avoid investigation.

NAZI:      We deny everything.
           But one of our lieutenants
           Has urgent business in Copenhagen,
           And cannot wait for the proper channels.
           The passport, please.

GERALD:    My fee, please –

*[He snaps his fingers in imitation of the NAZI.]*

           Five thousand Reichsmarks –

NAZI:      Do not be impatient.

GERALD:    Are Nazis the only ones allowed to be impatient?

*[NAZI produces a wallet and starts counting out 50 x 100 mark*

*notes. GERALD pushes his hands down, out of sight.]*

GERALD:        For heaven's sake! This is a public place.
                    If passers-by should see us,
                    They'll think we are suspicious.
                    Here – *[He snatches the money.]* I'll count it
                      later.

NAZI:            You trust a Nazi? Are you sure?

GERALD:        I do not need to trust you,
                    You wouldn't want me to shop you.
                    It would be so easy to bring you down.

NAZI:            I think in time we shall see
                    Who will bring who down.

GERALD:        You will always need fixers and movers like
                    me.

NAZI:            When we have the Third Reich
                    We will fix things for ourselves,
                    Herr Benson…

*[A formal bow. He exits. GERALD starts counting the high denomination notes.]*

GERALD:        One… two…. *[To audience:]* I wanted
                    dollars,
                  But they refuse to use Jewish money.

And I need the cash too much.
It is getting to the time to make an exit.

*[Lights fade on GERALD counting.]*

## Scene Eight

*[2nd February – 31st March 1933. The Moka Club again and various. The scene crosscuts rapidly, giving the impression of accelerating events, out of control. There has been a subtle change of atmosphere in the club. It is sombre, apprehensive. LOTTE's appearance is not light-hearted.]*

LOTTE:    When cold winds are blowing
And storm clouds are growing,
Cheer up! There's no need to be afeard.
You can put up an umbrella
If you find yourself a feller –
Get out and be sure to find a beard!

A beard can be terrific for transforming you,
So no-one is able to suspect.
It can shelter and hide you while it's
   warming you,
And no-one can possibly object.
Yes no-one can be harried
If their passport says they're married,
Cos for married couples, *Alles geht korrekt.*

So girls, if you've a lover,
Get a husband as a cover
And by the Gestapo you'll be cleared.
If you're homosexual,
The Nazis will not vex you all,
For no-one can argue with a beard.

We all will start to grow our girlish tresses.
Perhaps we'll tie them up in pretty bows.
Away with the suits! On with the dresses!
Sew on lots of frills and furbelows.
You can look like Theda Bara
Using hubby's best mascara.

If the brown shirts come a-knocking,
Wear your hubby's best silk stockings
And you'll see that no-one ever knows.

So girls, this may astound you,
But when you look around you.
All the lesbians will have disappeared.
For any girl that's mannish
Will have found a way to vanish,
Because she's found a way to grow a beard.

— But not a 'van Dyke' for heaven's sake.

*[She leaves the stage quickly without applause, lights fade. Up again as she enters hurriedly to PAULI.]*

LOTTE:       I cannot believe it. Hitler as Chancellor?!
             It is insane. We know what he will do,
             He has said it and written it a thousand
                times.
             Of course, we expect it of Hindenberg.
             The President is senile, he rambles all the
                time —

But those who advise him?
Those who finance him?
Are they so deluded to think they can
     control Hitler?

PAULI:          It will not be as bad as that,
                You are in shock at the news.
                I can't believe it is going to be
                As bad as you're predicting.

LOTTE:          It's going to be worse, far worse.
                Already they are starting the round-ups.
                They have closed the Moka Efti.
                They have smashed the windows
                Of Magnus Hirschfeld's Institute.

LOTTE:          It is the end of all Opposition,
                It is the end for people like us.
                Already they are building temporary camps,
                They make no secret of it.

PAULI:          We will be safe,
                Uncle Ernst will protect us.
                I know several of the boys
                Who have been with Rohm.
                Many of our kind have joined the SA,
                And the SA is two million strong.

LOTTE:          I must find my comrades.
                Shall we fight? Shall we go into exile?

I don't know what to do.

*[She exits. Quick crossfade of lights. GERALD comes to PAULI.]*

GERALD:     I must leave Germany at once,
            It is not safe to stay here.

PAULI:      Then I will come with you;
            You are my Friend,
            I have lived with you these six months.
            I can make a new life in England –
            Yes? – with you, with you.
            We will have a cottage in the country
            In Isleworth – that is your home, yes?
            I will cook steak and kidney pudding
            Just the way you like,
            And in the evening we will go to the pub,
            And drink beer and eat muffins outside.

*[GERALD is getting evasive.]*

GERALD:     Of course, you will need a passport.

PAULI:      You are right. There is no time to lose –
            You must help me. You have connections.

GERALD:     Perhaps, perhaps not. Not any more.

PAULI:      You have done so much for others,
            You can do it for me, I know.

GERALD:      I assure you I will try.

PAULI:       I know you can do it –
             You can do anything.
             You are my man, my friend,
             And I love you.

GERALD:      Yes, yes. *[He is distracted, irritated.]*

PAULI:       Do you love me?

*[GERALD looks deep into his eyes.]*

GERALD:      What do you think?

*[GERALD gives PAULI a quick peck on the forehead, or the arm, and makes a hasty exit. Quick crossfade of lights. Enter LOTTE.]*

LOTTE:       They have closed the KPD HQ.
             They say it will be the office
             Of the local Gauleiter.
             They are clearing it out.
             It is full of Brown Shirts
             Going through the papers.
             The Hitler Youth are burning
             Everything they can.

             Brecht has fled to Prague,
             Weill has gone to Paris.

I have been warned to flee,
But I wouldn't get a passport,
I am too well-known.

PAULI: Perhaps Gerald can get you a passport.
He's getting me a passport.
We can all live together
In Isleworth.

LOTTE: Pauli, stop dreaming. Be realistic.

Have you thought about what I said?
Will you marry me?
If we marry we can protect each other.
I can start performing for the Nazis –
People still need to be entertained.
They are opening new Nazi clubs
With happy, vacant songs.

PAULI: Could you do that?

LOTTE: If others can, I can.
Selli Engler wrote for the lesbian papers;
Now she's meant to be writing a play
In praise of Adolf Hitler.
Ruth Rolling put queer Berlin on the map
With her guide to lesbian bars.
Now she writes a novel against the Jews.

I could do it if I had to, to survive.
One day the Communists will return,
And I will be ready to join them.

Everything else will be idle gossip
If I am married to you.
I could even change my name –
Frau Gastern. Frau Lotte Gastern.
How does that sound?

*[A pause. PAULI is very conflicted.]*

PAULI:        I must go. I must go with my Friend,
              He will need me.

LOTTE:        And am I not your friend?
              Your oldest friend?
              Will you leave me to their mercy?

PAULI:        Come with us. Please.

LOTTE:        Gerald is not the altruist you think.
              He does not like women.
              He will not do it for me.

PAULI:        But I can ask. Please.

LOTTE:        I will not beg to men like Gerald.

PAULI:        *[Shouts]* But you will lick Hitler's arse!

*[Quick fade of lights. Lights up again on PAULI on his own, with a sheet of paper.]*

PAULI:     *[Reading]* My dearest Pauli,
        My sweet, sweet friend.
        There is no easy way to break this to you.
        To cut a long story short,
        I could not get a passport for you.

*[Light up on GERALD, whose voice joins in as a duet, and gradually takes over.]*

        I tried my damnedest, really I did.
        But the red tape is a nightmare,
        And will not take less than a month,
        Which I can ill afford.

*[PAULI visibly collapses like a burst balloon. He sobs silently, his shoulders heaving. GERALD solo, other lights slowly dimming to leave him in a single spot.]*

GERALD:     I have of course found passports in the past
        Through less orthodox channels,
        But circumstance has changed.
        My contacts are no more –
        Promoted to other offices,
        Or exiled to a camp.
        This is not the time to ask for favours.

So I will have to leave you.
I leave with the most sincere regret –
I wish it were not so, with all my heart,
And one day in a finer world
Maybe we'll be reunited
And have that cottage that we dreamed of.
You have been a precious, blessed friend
I will remember only with gratitude.
I will always carry you close to my heart,
Like your picture in my wallet.
Take care, my precious angel –
I will be thinking of you
And, I hope, watching over you.
Farewell, Pauli – or maybe au revoir.

*[GERALD takes PAULI's picture out of his wallet. Looks at it.]*

The conversation left a lot to be desired,
But the intercourse was bliss.

*[He tears up the photo and scatters the pieces. To audience:]*

What would you do?
How could I take him back to London?
They don't like foreigners in Isleworth.
Besides, I think my wife might object.

*[He goes through his pockets, produces two passports. Weighs between the two.]*

Gerald Hamilton… Cosmo Fanshawe…
I rather like the name Cosmo.
New name, new phase, new life.

*[He chucks 'Gerald Hamilton' into a bin. He picks up his suitcase and exits. A change of lights. Wedding music. PAULI and LOTTE enter solemnly dressed as bride and groom. They turn upstage and freeze. As they do so, the NAZI from before, now a high official in the Interior Ministry, steps into a spotlight. He is looking intently at the sheets of paper which GERALD handed to the APPARATCHIK a year earlier. There is a note attached to the front of them by paper clip. He peers at this to try and identify illegible handwriting. Slowly, spoken:]*

NAZI:          Pauli… Gastern…

*[He produces a notebook and writes the name in it.]*

                  Pauli… Gastern…

*[He looks at the paper again. Decisive, brutal:]*

                  Pauli Gastern.

*[He takes the paper and crushes it in his hand. The music swells discordantly, a herald of what is to come. Adolf Hitler's first speech to the Reichstag as Chancellor in February 1933 rises slowly to full volume.[5]]*

---

[5] https://archive.org/details/HitlerSpeechSportpalast1933EntireSpeechMissing
PartsReAdded

SNAP BLACKOUT

THE END

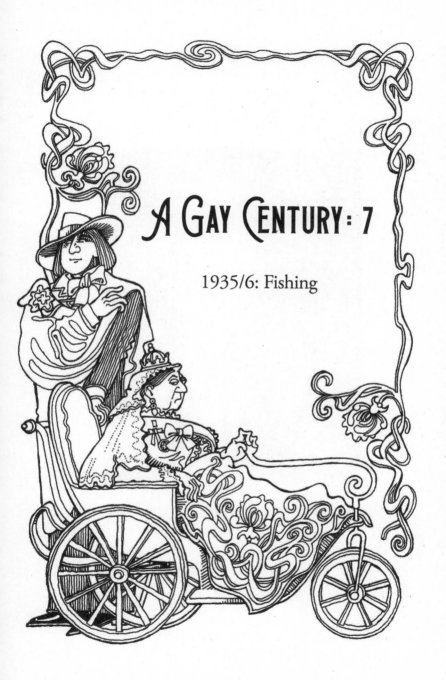

# A GAY CENTURY: 7

## 1935/6: Fishing

Above: *Lord Alfred Douglas, by Howard Coster, 1940s. NPG collection*

# INTRODUCTION

*Fishing* was the first chamber opera libretto I wrote, before I had any idea about this huge cycle. My friend Andrew Lumsden, activist, co-founder and later editor of *Gay News*, painter, historian and all-round good thing, gave me the story.

A friend of his, older than he, turned eighty around the Millennium, and he told Andrew how, as a teenager, he had met Lord Alfred Douglas, then in his sixties. When his mother learned of this, she forbade the boy to speak to him again, with the result that he snubbed Douglas without really understanding why. Andrew said that what had struck him was that his friend still felt guilt about the way he'd treated Douglas over sixty years later.

I saw immediately that this had the kind of shape that would fit an opera – a simple but strong story, a clear line of development, four well-defined characters (Andrew's friend is split in two, the young and the old self). I could also see parallels with Benjamin Britten – the haunted Captain Vere in *Billy Budd*; or, alternatively, *Death in Venice* seen from the young Tadzio's point of view.

I was also intrigued by the character of Douglas, a nasty piece of work by anybody's standards. He turned on his old friends, dragged Wilde's name through the mud ['the greatest force for evil that has appeared in Europe for the last 350 years'], and drove his love-rival Robbie Ross to his death. Add that he was a virulent anti-Semite, litigator and bearer of grudges. And yet towards the end of his life he began, in his own way, to soften and make amends.

Douglas's tragedy is two-fold: firstly, that the most momentous events of his life occurred before he was thirty, and he spend the last forty-five years of his life trying to find a talent and a place in the world that would be worthy of his past; he never did. Secondly, he dragged with him everywhere his 'notorious' reputation, our most famous homosexual, 'The Vilest Man in Britain' in today's parlance. What does that do to a man's psychology, especially a man who has become a fervent Catholic?

Guilt is passed on from generation to generation, from Douglas to Philip (as I call him). It echoes down the ages, born out of repression, self-denial, hypocrisy and ignorance. Oscar's legacy takes many forms, and lingers long; in this case, into a new millennium.

Sources: *Lord Alfred Douglas* by H Montgomery Hyde [Methuen 1984]

*Bosie: Lord Alfred Douglas, his friends and enemies* by Rupert Croft-Cook [WH Allen 1963]

*Bosie* by Douglas Murray [Sceptre 2001]

*My Friendship with Oscar Wilde* by Lord Alfred Douglas [Coventry House 1932]

# CAST

**ALFRED DOUGLAS** : Tenor
*65-ish. Shrivelled, wrinkled, bulbous white nose. No trace of the great beauty of the 1890s. His costume would have been considered old-fashioned even in the mid-1930s – wing collar like Neville Chamberlain's, maybe tweeds. [NB. There should be no hint that this is Oscar Wilde's lover; the audience should discover it at the same time as Philip's mother – see script.] He occasionally uses words which have a double meaning, but he has no awareness of this fact, and their use is entirely innocent.*

**OLD PHILIP** : Baritone
*79, frail. A rug over his knees, a book of poems in his hand. A hint in the lighting of a flickering fire.*

**YOUNG PHILIP** : Countertenor
*14-ish, handsome. He is on holiday. Short-sleeved Fair Isle sweater, shorts.*

**MRS DALTON** : Mezzo
*40s, a working single mother, slightly harassed. [Philip's father is dead.]*

# SETTING

A bare stage, with four chairs at the corners of what might be a boxing ring. A piano aside from them. The action takes place in the year 2000, but then in memory returns to 1935/6. Period indicated by costume.

I envisage this being played in the round, though it is not essential. The singers all sit in the chairs, and come forward into the scene as required, with the exception of OLD PHILIP, who stays sitting throughout. Hand props are kept by the convenient chair.

INSTRUMENTS

Piano, violin, cello

FISHING

*[Spotlight on OLD PHILIP. He struggles to read, gives up, stares into the fire. It flickers and fades.]*

OLD PHILIP:    The fire flickers –
I cannot see to read any more.
It fades,
As transient and fitful as memory.
But memories return…
The pier. Waves below.
A bobbing hook. The swaying line.

*[Over these last two lines YOUNG PHILIP takes up position, fishing rod in hand, on Brighton Pier, a small bucket at his feet.]*

DOUGLAS:    *[Distant, from his chair:]* Won't you say
hello?
Won't you say hello?

*[Over OLD PHILIP's lines he comes forward to YOUNG PHILIP.]*

OLD PHILIP:    I can never forget him,
Never forgive him.
Never forgive myself.

I read poems from his book every day,
And always in my mind I hear him…
See him…

DOUGLAS:         What ho! Fishing again, young fellow-
                 me-lad?

YOUNG PHILIP:    Sir?

DOUGLAS:         I saw you here yesterday,
                 I've been watching you all week.
                 Do you like fishing? *[Pause]*

MRS DALTON:      *[From her chair:]* Answer the question,
                 Speak when spoken to.

YOUNG PHILIP:    Yes sir.

DOUGLAS:         I thought you must.
                 You seem to catch so few,
                 Yet still you come.

YOUNG PHILIP:    I like it very much.
                 You can lose yourself in looking at
                     the waves.
                 And no-one bothers you.

DOUGLAS:         Am I bothering you?

MRS. D:          Answer the question.
                 Speak when spoken to.

YOUNG PHILIP:    Not at all.
                 Thank you, sir.

                        But today I've caught nothing.

DOUGLAS:            So I see.
                    How long have you been here?
                    Here on the pier today?

YOUNG PHILIP:       Three hours, sir.

DOUGLAS:            So long, and still an empty bucket.
                    It's all in the wrist and forearm, you
                        know.

YOUNG PHILIP:       What is?

DOUGLAS:            The secret of success.
                    I know something about it,
                    I'm something of a fly fisherman.

YOUNG PHILIP:       You, sir?

DOUGLAS:            Believe me.
                    The slippery speckled trout, the crafty
                        pike,
                    Hidden in the reeds.
                    Silvery salmon; carp, queen of rivers.
                    Each with its ways,
                    Each a challenge,
                    And a strategy for each.
                    Mostly rivers and lakes of course,
                    But the principle's the same.

YOUNG PHILIP:    Really? Oh teach me, sir,
                 I long to take a big fish home
                 For our supper,
                 To please my mother.

DOUGLAS:         From here, from the pier,
                 You need a forward cast.
                 The rod, a lever, gives energy to the
                     line.
                 Let me show you. See...

*[He leans over the boy, his hands over the boy's. He pulls the rod in an arc overhead, until it's parallel with the ground behind them, and then flicks it high overhead so the line spins out a distance. This is conveyed by their eyes – there is no line on the rod.]*

YOUNG PHILIP:    Gracious heavens!
                 I've never put it out so far before.

DOUGLAS:         What is your bait, lad?

YOUNG PHILIP:    Sandworms, sir.

DOUGLAS:         No good – they disintegrate.
                 You need a pheasant tail nymph,
                 Or some poppers or a woolly bugger,
                 All good flies, and sturdy.
                 I still have some, I think –
                 I can bring them if you like.

YOUNG PHILIP:     Would you sir? That's very kind.

DOUGLAS:          Now let's see you do it for yourself.
                  Remember what I said,
                  It's all in the wrist and forearm.
                  So pull it back… And over…
                  And flick… and stop!
                  Bravo! Well done!

OLD PHILIP:       All afternoon I cast and hauled,
                  And made another cast.
                  And I caught fish!
                  The sun blazed down, and slowly bent
                  Towards the west.

DOUGLAS:          Well done again. How many is that
                      now?

YOUNG PHILIP:     Five, sir.

DOUGLAS:          That's very good off Brighton Pier.

YOUNG PHILIP:     I can't wait to write to tell Freddie.
                  That's my brother, sir.

DOUGLAS:          I think you've earned some tea.
                  My treat. And a Chelsea Bun.

YOUNG PHILIP:     Oh yes, please, sir. I'm ravenous.

DOUGLAS: In that case we will have a slap-up spread.

*[At this point the music becomes a love duet to food.]*

Eclairs and French fancies –

YOUNG PHILIP: And doughnuts and cream slices –

DOUGLAS: Cream slices! How I love cream slices!

YOUNG PHILIP: So do I!

DOUGLAS: How about cream horns?

YOUNG PHILIP: Oh yes.

DOUGLAS: And scones *[rhymes with bones]* with raspberry jam.

YOUNG PHILIP: You mean scones. *[Rhymes with dons]*

DOUGLAS: Yes, scones. *[Rhymes with bones]*

YOUNG PHILIP: And cream?

DOUGLAS: Of course. How are you on cake?

YOUNG PHILIP: I love cake.

DOUGLAS:        And I. Victoria sponge –

YOUNG PHILIP:    With cream. And jam.

DOUGLAS/YOUNG PHILIP:
                And rich moist fruit cake. – Mmmmm!

DOUGLAS:        Then come with me.
                We'll stop at a little baker I know.
                I have a small studio in a basement
                In Nizell's Avenue in Hove.

*[Lights change. They travel across stage. Pull up their chairs in the middle. Lounge to suggest they are easy chairs.]*

OLD PHILIP:     In those days we were trusting,
                We did what grown-ups told us.
                We believed what they said,
                We did as we were told.

*[Lights change onto the middle. Mellow atmosphere. Tea and cream cakes.]*

DOUGLAS:        Where are you at school, Philip?

YOUNG PHILIP:    Lancing, sir. I have a scholarship.
                My father's dead.

DOUGLAS:        Oh! Rotten show!

YOUNG PHILIP:     *[Ashamed]* We're rather poor.

DOUGLAS:          Me too…
                  I was at Winchester.
                  We used to play you at cricket.
                  Do you like it? Lancing, I mean.

YOUNG PHILIP:     Yes sir. I don't like cricket.

DOUGLAS:          Nor did I. Another cake?

YOUNG PHILIP:     I couldn't.

DOUGLAS:          What? A growing lad like you? Go on.

*[PHILIP takes another cake.]*

                  So, what do you like most at Lancing?

YOUNG PHILIP:     I like languages the best. Italian, French.
                  But German I hate.

DOUGLAS:          So do I. Filthy language, filthy people.
                  Though Hitler is right about the Jews.

YOUNG PHILIP:     I think Hitler's a rotten egg!

DOUGLAS:          Do you now? Well, let's not quarrel.
                  I speak French quite well, you know –
                  I translated from the French.

Have you heard of Salome?

YOUNG PHILIP:    Of course. She's in the bible.
                She did a dance for Herod.

DOUGLAS:        So she did. With seven veils.
                That was never in the Bible,
                It was in our play – we invented it –
                *[He stops himself.]*
                Would you like to speak French?
                *Nous pouvons parler en français si vous
                voulez.*

YOUNG PHILIP:    *[Shudders]* Ugh. No thank you, sir.
                I'm on holiday.

DOUGLAS:        What else do you like?

YOUNG PHILIP:    I like –

DOUGLAS:        Yes?

YOUNG PHILIP:    *[Hesitant, almost ashamed]* I like
                poetry, sir.

DOUGLAS:        You make it sound a filthy habit,
                Like picking your nose.

YOUNG PHILIP:    It's just that – well – the other chaps
                Make fun of me.

They're more keen on sport and
    stuff.

DOUGLAS:        Ah! Rise above them.
                You are better far than they.
                The soul of the artist is purest alabaster,
                And wreathed in precious amarynths.

YOUNG PHILIP:    I'm not an artist –

DOUGLAS:        But you will be, you will be.
                You show all the signs –
                You are sensitive to poetry and
                    beauty…

YOUNG PHILIP:    Sometimes, when I'm fishing
                And I'm getting bored,
                I say poems to myself.

DOUGLAS:        *[Shyly]* Could you say one to me?

YOUNG PHILIP:    No!

DOUGLAS:        Why not?

YOUNG PHILIP:    It's soppy.

DOUGLAS:        No! No! Never!
                It is a proud escutcheon,
                A blazon of superiority

Of intellect, perception and of soul.
Like liquid amber on the breath,
Both sword and shield
Against the world's hostility.

Go on. Say one. For me.

YOUNG PHILIP:　　*[Thinks for a moment, then takes a*
　　　　　　　　　　*deep breath:]*
　　　　　　　　So, we'll go no more a roving
　　　　　　　　So late into the night,
　　　　　　　　Though the heart is still as loving
　　　　　　　　And the moon be still as bright.

　　　　　　　　For – for – er – I can't remember…

DOUGLAS:　　For the sword outwears its sheath
　　　　　　　　And the soul wears out the breast…

YOUNG PHILIP:　　And the soul wears out the breast,
　　　　　　　　And the heart must pause to – pause
　　　　　　　　to –

DOUGLAS:　　Breathe.
　　　　　　　　And love itself have rest.

DOUGLAS/YOUNG PHILIP:
　　　　　　　　Though the night was made for loving
　　　　　　　　And the day returns too soon,
　　　　　　　　Yet we'll go no more a-roving

By the light of the moon.

*[Over the last two lines, DOUGLAS touches the boy's hair. This is distant, dreamy, and not sexual.]*

DOUGLAS:        *[Soft, to himself]*
                Such beauty, such beauty…
                Beauteous angel,
                Hair, spun gold…
                Rich lips, carnation red,
                And skin of ivory, white and smooth
                    and fine…
                Once I was such a one:
                I was beloved once.

YOUNG PHILIP:   Sir?

DOUGLAS:        You recite very prettily. Byron, was it
                    not?
                They called him 'Mad, bad and danger-
                    ous to know.'
                And so he was. An irreligious libertine.
                But such beauty he could make…

YOUNG PHILIP:   What's a libertine, sir?

DOUGLAS:        A libertine?
                A man who lives but for himself,
                And for the whim of pleasure,
                And doesn't go to church.

Do you go to church?

YOUNG PHILIP: To chapel, sir.

DOUGLAS: But do you *believe* in it?

YOUNG PHILIP: I don't know, sir. I've been having
doubts.

DOUGLAS: But you must, you must.
It was the making and saving of me,
And so it will be for you.
You see, I recognise the sickness in your
soul...
I – *[pause]* I am a poet too, you know.

YOUNG PHILIP: Really? Would I know your poems?

DOUGLAS: I doubt it. Perhaps when you are older –

*[Pause. He comes to a decision.]*

I'd like you to have something.
Perhaps it will speak to you.

YOUNG PHILIP: Something for me?

DOUGLAS: From me to you. Why not?
I sense a fellow feeling,
The soul of an artist.

*[He goes to the chair of the sleeping OLD PHILIP and takes the book of poems from his lap.]*

>Here. Let me inscribe it.
>*[Writes]* To Philip...
>To one who dreams,
>And longs for what he cannot have,
>From another fervid seeker after truth.
>Your friend... etc. etc.
>
>Here.

*[He hands the book to YOUNG PHILIP.]*

YOUNG PHILIP:     Oh sir, you are too kind.

DOUGLAS:     I think we can advance beyond 'sir' now,
Don't you? Call me Alfred.

YOUNG PHILIP:     I shall cherish it always – *[shyly]*
Alfred.

DOUGLAS:     And now it is nearly six o'clock,
And I must go to Mass. *[He pronounces
it 'Maas']*
And you to the bosom of your loving
family.

YOUNG PHILIP:     Only my mother sir.
Freddie's off at Scout Camp.

DOUGLAS:       But she will wonder where you are,
               And she will want that fish.
               Where do you live?

YOUNG PHILIP:    In Ovingdean.

DOUGLAS:       There is a bus along the sea front.
               When I was your age, we had a goat
                   cart,
               My sister and I –

YOUNG PHILIP:    What's a goat cart?

DOUGLAS:       A little cart pulled by a goat,
               They were all the rage in Brighton.
               I miss them. Here –

*[He fishes in his pocket, pulls out a coin.]*

               That will pay your fare home.
               Now don't forget your rod and line –
               And your fish. And your book.
               Now go.

*[He shoos YOUNG PHILIP out. Turns out his pockets.]*

               And that's the last till my wife Olive sends
               My next allowance.
               To live on scraps like these!
               No more bets on horses now for me.

Hey ho…

*[Lights change. An old-fashioned doorbell of the kind that rings when a door is opened. MRS DALTON comes to centre stage.]*

MRS DALTON:     Philip, is that you? Where have you
                been?

YOUNG PHILIP:   *[Rushing in]* Sorry, mother, but you'll
                not believe –
                Look, I've caught some fish.

MRS DALTON:     So you have. Lovely!
                We'll have those for our tea.
                That's come at the right time,
                There's nothing in the house.

YOUNG PHILIP:   You have them, I'm not hungry.

MRS DALTON:     Look at you –
                Jam all round your mouth.
                What have you been eating?

YOUNG PHILIP:   Scones. *[He pronounces it the
                DOUGLAS way.]*

MRS DALTON:     'Scones', is it?!
                Where did you learn to speak all posh
                like that?

YOUNG PHILIP:     And jam. And éclairs. And cream
                  horns.
                  He took me to his flat in Hove for
                  tea.

MRS DALTON:     Who did?

YOUNG PHILIP:     He taught me how to cast a line as
                  well.
                  You just flick your wrist like this –

                  *[He does so. It looks slightly fey.]*

                  It's easy when you know.

MRS DALTON:     Who did?

YOUNG PHILIP:     I met this nice man on the pier,
                  He took me home to tea.
                  He was ever so interesting. He's a
                  poet.
                  He gave me some of his poems.
                  Look!

*[He fishes out the book of poems.]*

                  He signed it for me. See!

*[MRS DALTON reads. She mouths the words, DOUGLAS sings them from his seat.]*

DOUGLAS: To Philip,
To one who dreams,
And longs for what he cannot have.

*[The voice segues into MRS DALTON's — there is a brief overlap.]*

MRS DALTON: From another fervid seeker after truth,
Your friend... Alfred Douglas.

*[DOUGLAS joins in this from his seat. MRS DALTON turns the page over.]*

MRS DALTON: Sonnets of Lord Alfred Douglas.
Oh, oh! Saints preserve us!
Filthy! Abominable! Filthy!

*[She tries to tear up the book, which proves obstinately durable.]*

What did he do to you?
Did he touch you?
Did he try to put his hands
On – ?
If he laid a finger on you
I'll kill him, so help me.
What did he do to you?

YOUNG PHILIP: Nothing. He did nothing at all.
He taught me how to cast my rod
And gave me tea.

MRS DALTON:     Disgusting! Disgusting!

*[She is literally frothing. She tries to tear the book with her teeth. In desperation:]*

MRS DALTON:     Bring me some matches. I'll burn this
                evil book.

YOUNG PHILIP:   It's only poems. Poems can't be evil.

MRS DALTON:     You see? Already he's corrupted you.
                Take your clothes off!

*[She attempts to rip the clothes off PHILIP's body.]*

YOUNG PHILIP:   Stop it, mother. You're hurting me.

MRS DALTON:     I'm going to give you a good scrubbing
                all over.
                I'll wash his evil out of you.

YOUNG PHILIP:   What has he done?

MRS DALTON:     Never you mind what he's done.
                He did it, and that's enough.
                Now promise me
                You'll never ever talk to him again.

YOUNG PHILIP:   What has he done?

MRS DALTON:     Promise me. Swear on your father's
                grave.

YOUNG PHILIP:   But if he comes along the pier –

MRS DALTON:     Then don't go to the pier.

YOUNG PHILIP:   I must go to the pier.

MRS DALTON:     Why must you go to the pier?
                You want to see him, don't you?
                He has corrupted you,
                But I forbid it – do you understand?

YOUNG PHILIP:   Yes, mother.

MRS DALTON:     Then swear. Swear!

YOUNG PHILIP:   *[Grumbling]* All right. I swear.

MRS DALTON:     What do you swear?

YOUNG PHILIP:   I swear I'll never talk
                To Alfred any more.

MRS DALTON:     'Alfred', is it? This is worse than I
                thought.
                Come with me to the bathroom.

*[She grabs him and tugs him off the stage.]*

We'll run a bath and scrub you clean.
And burn this rotten filth.

YOUNG PHILIP:    But what's he done? What has he
                 done?

*[Lights change. OLD PHILIP again.]*

OLD PHILIP:      She never did explain. All she would say
                 was —

MRS DALTON:      If you don't know, then I'm not telling
                 you,
                 And putting ideas into your head.

*[They exit, and the voices fade. Spotlight on OLD PHILIP.]*

OLD PHILIP:      Oh how I longed to see that man again.
                 To hear his talk,
                 And eat his scones with jam and cream.
                 But I had sworn, on father's grave,
                 And that was a mighty oath.

                 She could not burn the book,
                 The cover would not take the flame.
                 In summer there was no fire
                 To burn it on.
                 I rescued it when her back was turned,
                 And hid it in the garden shed.

I did not see him again that holiday,
Although I thought about him often.
Term came round. Lower Fourth.
Football, hockey, fives,
And no escape.
I fell in love with Clayton Minor
And no escape.

The year passed,
The sun shone again,
Fred Perry had won Wimbledon,
Soon there'd be Olympics in Berlin,
And I was on the pier once more in
    Brighton.

*[Lights change. Sound of the sea. YOUNG PHILIP again on the pier, with his fishing rod. He casts more expertly. DOUGLAS approaches, watches with satisfaction.]*

DOUGLAS:        Hello, young fellow-me-lad. What ho!
                It's Philip, ain't it?

*[There is no reaction. DOUGLAS gradually through this realises that something is wrong, and his joviality appears more and more to be whistling in the dark.]*

                I was sorry not to see you again last
                    year.
                Our little feast quite laid me low,
                Too rich for my sad stomach.

No more cream éclairs for me!

*[Pause for reaction. There is none.]*

You learnt your lesson well, I see.
That flick of the wrist – very good, very
good.
And how is school? How is Lancing?

*[No reaction.]*

Have you learnt any good poems this
year?
Perhaps – you have learned – one of
mine…

*[Still waiting for a reaction. There is none. YOUNG PHILIP keeps his head down, looking at the sea below, but we can see from his rigid back that he is well aware of what is going on. Music here echoes his mother's injunctions.]*

DOUGLAS:      Don't you remember me? I gave you
tea,
And taught you how to use your wrist
To get the nymph to fly, the line spin
out.
We had éclairs, remember? And French
fancies,
Doughnuts and cream slices.

*[Another pause. YOUNG PHILIP turns his back more firmly. DOUGLAS can be in no doubt. An outburst:]*

DOUGLAS:  Not you too, Philip?
God, why must you punish me?
Still you punish me for forty years ago.
What more can I do? I joined the
    church,
Repent my sins each day, go to mass
And say confession.
I have confessed the sin of unkindness,
Atoned for Oscar, my slanders
And my feuds with Frank Harris.
I made my peace with Robbie Ross at
    last.
I wrote of Oscar's greatness, not his
    weakness.
What more can I do?
Sweet Jesus, take this burden from my
    shoulders,
This everlasting loneliness and shame.

*[To PHILIP:]*  I never did you harm, my boy – did I?
I only fed you cakes and wished you
    well,
My only sin the sin of envy of your
    youth.
What did I do, Philip? What did I do?
The least that being a gentleman
    demands

Is, tell me what I did to you.

*[Still obstinate silence. DOUGLAS recognises PHILIP is determined to avoid him, so he makes a very formal, old-fashioned bow.]*

DOUGLAS:    I thought I recognised
            A soul of purest alabaster.
            I was mistaken.
            It has been soiled.
            At least I knew an *artist* when I saw
                one.

*[He exits. As he goes, an echo, a cry to the world:]*
            Is there no forgiveness, is there no end
                to it?

*[A lights change. OLD PHILIP by the fire.]*

OLD PHILIP:  An artist? Ha! How I wish I was!
            But war and building the New Jerus-
                alem
            Put paid to all those fancy daydreams.
            To build a hospital was more important
            Than writing a sonnet. Or learning one.

            I saw his death in the papers –
            1945. I was in the RAF, aged twenty-
                four,
            And lost my heart to an aircraftsman,

Second class.

It was not true that I forgot him.
I never ceased to think of him,
A sad old shrivelled man, kind to me,
Whose kindness I repaid with learned
    contempt.

Perhaps if I had joined the church
I would have found forgiveness
And a kind of peace.
But I could not. And did not.

Sometimes it was good:–

DOUGLAS:      *[From his chair]* You must rise above
                  them,
              You are better far than they.

OLD PHILIP:   That stood me in good stead
              With the hatred of the world
              For me and all my kind
              Fifty years ago.
              But mostly I have been bowed
              Beneath the burden of guilt;
              It pressed on me.

              Death comes. I see his shadow fall.
              I thought it would dissolve all things.
              But at the last the guilt still crushes me.

I knew no better –
That is all that I can plead.
And I believed
What grown-ups told me.

MRS DALTON:     *[From her chair:]* Answer the question –
Speak when spoken to –
Do what you are told.

DOUGLAS:        Come with me...
Come with me...

*[This is a kind of musical battle between MRS DALTON and DOUGLAS in the background from their seats.]*

DOUGLAS:        Such beauty, such beauty...

MRS DALTON:     Burn this rotten filth!

DOUGLAS:        Rise above it,
We must both rise above it.

MRS DALTON:     Filthy! Abominable!

*[Her interjections fade, leaving the duet:]*

OLD P/DOUGLAS:  Though the night was made for
loving
And the day returns too soon,
Yet we'll go no more a-roving

By the light of the moon.

*[OLD PHILIP slumps in the chair. Fade to* Blackout.]

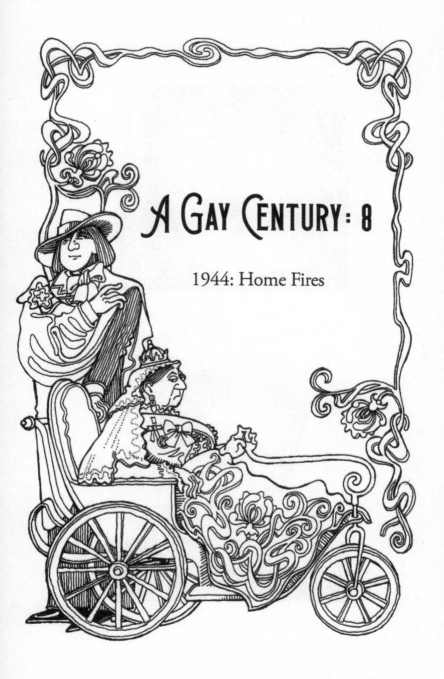

# A Gay Century: 8

### 1944: Home Fires

Above: *Ivor Novello*
Below: *Frankie Fraser, 1956*

# INTRODUCTION

It's funny how you mishear things when you're only half listening. Once in the early 80s I was wrestling with a newspaper column close to a deadline, with the radio playing in the background. I was startled to hear on the news that fighting had broken out in Debenham's. And it wasn't even the first day of the Sales. The newsreader had, of course, said 'Lebanon', in an item about Israeli aggression against its Arab neighbour.

I was reminded of this when, half-listening to Radio 3 while working on the libretto for *Two Queens*, I heard Matthew Sweet talking in a slot called *Time Travellers*, where some quirky little historical morsel with a musical connection was briefly aired by a guest. He was telling the fascinating story of how Ivor Novello, golden boy of British musical theatre of the 30s and 40s and the prettiest man in England, was sent to prison for fiddling his petrol coupons during World War II. It almost certainly cost him his knighthood.

At the time no-one was allowed petrol unless they were doing work of national importance. Novello pleaded that he needed his monogrammed Rolls Royce because he was boosting national morale, but to no avail. Enter Grace Constable, a besotted fan, who overheard him at the stage door lamenting that he couldn't motor down to his place in Maidenhead at the weekends – he held regular orgies there. To ingratiate herself with him, Grace suggested that he should lend her firm the car, they would get petrol and use it in the week, and he could go off with it at the weekends.

It was a cheeky suggestion from a typist under a false name pretending to be far more important in the company than she was. They knew nothing of it when the fraud was discovered, and Novello had the misfortune to come before a magistrate who hated musicals and homosexuals with an equal passion. As a result he got 28 days in Wandsworth Prison – where Oscar Wilde had been incarcerated in 1894 between Pentonville and Reading Gaol, and where he got the ear infection which hastened his death.

Matthew Sweet said – and I may have misheard this – that he interviewed 'Mad' Frankie Fraser, psychopathic sidekick and bully boy of the Richardson gang. In the 60s, Charlie and Eddie Richardson ran one of the most violent criminal set-ups in London, second only to the Kray Twins. Pulling out fingernails with pliers and cutting off toes with bolt cutters was a Fraser speciality. Fraser claimed, according to Sweet, that he briefly shared a cell with Ivor Novello. I nearly fell out of my chair.

And it got better. Again according to Fraser/Sweet, Novello was very distressed at being in prison, and nervous of meeting the other inmates, but as he was going down to lunch from his cell on the first day, all the prisoners lined up and sang *We'll Gather Lilacs* to welcome him. That clinched it. In my mind I heard the humming chorus from *Madama Butterfly*. There had to be an opera in it.

That was the moment when the complete project of *A Gay Century* came swimming into focus. We had 1900, 1918 and 1935/6 – and now here was 1944. Later I realised that this story couldn't be entirely true, to say the least. Novello's second most popular song, from *Perchance to Dream*, didn't see the light of day until 1945, a year after his imprisonment, so there was no way that the cons could have known it. On the other hand, they would have known *Keep the Home Fires Burning*....

I read Fraser's self-serving memoirs, all three volumes of them. He claims acquaintance with Novello, but no more; he also denies knowing that Novello was gay, which from someone who spent nearly half his life in the nick, with all the goings-on which that implies, is frankly incredible. He seems the kind of 'celebrity rough' who would tell anyone in the media what they wanted to hear. But still, it was too good to let go. The problem was, what could connect the effete, dreamy theatre queen with the tough spiv with a penchant for inflicting pain?

I decided that the clue had to be in Fraser's prospective hospital treatment. The authorities had decided he was so uncontrollable, so irredeemable, that he needed some form of shock treatment to subdue him. He was to be sent to Banstead Asylum for ECT[6]. For any gay man, aversion therapy of this kind would have been part of the daily terror in which they lived at the time; many who came up before the beak for importuning or gross indecency would agree to have ECT or drug therapy ('chemical castration') to avoid longer prison sentences. They knew not what they were letting themselves in for, but their stories of their torture after the event went the rounds of their friends. It loomed enormous in the collective

---

[6] Electroconvulsive Therapy

gay conscious. Ivor would have known people who had been on the receiving end, though his natural bent for escaping anything unpleasant would not have allowed him to dwell on the subject.

To this great encounter I added Ivor's weird and wonderful mother, Clara, who had died a year previously. I needed someone he could confess to. She was a music teacher and voice coach, and ran a strange outfit called the Welsh Grandmothers' Choir. She was convinced that these Welsh Grannies were destined for stardom and would bring World Peace. Ivor spent much of his life bailing her out financially from these disastrous escapades.

This opera is the first in which Queen Victoria does not appear either literally or figuratively; both Ivor and Frankie are implicitly opposed to Victorian values. However, the connection to Wilde, through the prison itself, carries on the theme of the contiguous and collective gay experience throughout the century. And we are not finished with Wilde even yet, as you will see.

Sources: *Mad Frank's Underworld History of Britain* by Frankie Fraser with James Morton [Virgin 2007]
*Mad Frank and Friends* by Frank Fraser with James Morton [Little, Brown 1998]
*Mad Frank's Diary* by Frank Fraser with James Morton [Virgin 2000]
*The Painted King* by Rhys Davies [Heinemann 1954]
*Ivor Novello* by James Harding [Welsh Academic Press 1997]

*Ivor Novello: Story of an Achievement* by WJ Mac-Queen-Pope [Hutchinson 1954]
*Noël Coward: A Biography* by Philip Hoare [Sinclair-Stevenson 1995]
*The Happy Hoofer* by Celia Imrie [Hodder & Stoughton 2011]

# CAST

**IVOR NOVELLO** : Tenor
*An extremely handsome and well-preserved man of fifty. Pampered, sheltered and childish, but generous. Used to seducing in all kinds of ways. Very soft attractive voice.*

**FRANKIE FRASER** : Baritone
*A good-looking lad of 20, but dangerous. Destined to become a violent criminal, he will go on to spend 42 years in prison. More than a touch of the psycho.*

**MRS CLARA NOVELLO-DAVIES** : Soprano
*Ivor Novello's mother. A large blowsy woman, self-dramatising, alcoholic, smothering. (She died about a year before this, aged 82, so she is in his memory.)*

**WARDER** : Bass
*Prison Officer, stolid, smart and uniformed. Shows some deference to Ivor's celebrity status and real hostility to Frankie.*

# SETTING

It is 18th May 1944. A drab cell at Wandsworth Prison. A bare bench. Plain dim lighting.

# INSTRUMENTS

Harp, alto and tenor saxophones

# HOME FIRES

*[The WARDER shows IVOR into his cell. He is wearing a loose
shabby grey jacket and trousers – prison clothes.]*

WARDER:     This is your cell.

IVOR:     *[Dismayed]* Thank you.

WARDER:     Don't worry, you'll get used to it.
It's only a month.

IVOR:     *[Shaken]* May I have a cigarette?

WARDER:     Sorry, Mr Novello,
I'm not allowed.
Perhaps your friends can bring you some –
You can have visitors soon.
Bear up,
It's just a matter of will power.

*[WARDER leaves – closing the door firmly.]*

IVOR:     Oh the shame!
My reputation is ruined.
I have filled Drury Lane
For nearly ten years –
Oh the shame! –
Night after night
With music and romance:

*Glamorous Night –*
*Careless Rapture –*
*The Dancing Years!*

Who will want to see me now?
Nothing but a common felon –
Look at me!
What do I look like?
I came in here dressed like a gentleman,
Double breasted Glen Plain suit,
Shirt from Jermyn Street,
Silk tie, and handkerchief
In the top breast pocket,
Straight from the Court of London Ses-
    sions.
Not even pyjamas!
I will miss my silk pyjamas…

I need a cigarette…
This craving is torture.

Oh Mam, I have let you down
So badly, so badly.
I'm so glad you didn't live to see this.

CLARA:        *[Off-stage]* Oh Ivor,
          I will always live
          In your memory.

*[CLARA appears.]*

All my life I lived for you,
And now I live in you.

IVOR:      I am so ashamed.

CLARA:     You have nothing to be ashamed of.
           That dreadful common typist
           Took advantage of you.
           She was in love with you.

IVOR:      Grace Walton?

CLARA:     Constable. Not Walton, Grace Constable.
           She used a phoney name
           So she could con you.

IVOR:      She was not in love with me.

CLARA:     Oh Ivor, *everyone* falls in love with you.

IVOR:      *[Sighs]* I know. It is a great bore.

CLARA:     My poor boy. Come here.

*[She cradles his head in her ample bosom.]*

           She lied to you,
           Promised you could keep your car
           To use at weekends,
           While her company would own it

|  |  |
|---|---|
|  | And get the petrol. |
| IVOR: | I didn't understand what was going on. |
| CLARA: | Of course you never understood.<br>You were made for fairy tale and fantasy –<br>What would you know of petrol coupons? |
| IVOR: | I tried, Mam,<br>To get my own coupons.<br>I told them I was doing work<br>Of national importance. |
| CLARA: | Of course you were;<br>You were keeping up morale. |
| IVOR: | They turned me down. |
| CLARA: | This wretched war!<br>If I had had my way<br>It would never have happened! |
| IVOR: | *[Protesting]* Oh Mam… |
| CLARA: | I should have sung for Hitler.<br>I was all ready to go to Berlin<br>With my Welsh Grandmothers' Choir<br>To sing for him.<br>I would have changed his mind<br>With the power of music. |

IVOR:  Don't fret, darling.
       It's over now,
       There's nothing to be done.
       Peace, peace, darling.

*[She turns and slowly fades from view.]*

CLARA:  *[Off-stage]* Bear up, Ivor.
        Be strong, be proud,
        A son of the Valleys.

*[IVOR is left alone. He is twitchy without cigarettes. The WARDER opens the door and pushes FRANKIE in.]*

WARDER:  Get back in there Fraser –
         And watch yourself.

FRANKIE:  Fuck off, screw.

WARDER:  I'll have you.

FRANKIE:  How? I got no privileges to lose.

WARDER:  One morning, when you're slopping out,
         Me and some mates, get you in a corner...
         You'll feel it.

FRANKIE:  You and whose army?
          I can take you all down.
          I just done a screw in Feltham

For having a go at me
About me stitching.

WARDER:    And what good did that do you?
Got you here.
And now they're going to fry your brain, ha!

*[FRANKIE is about to clock the WARDER, but IVOR intervenes.]*

IVOR:    *[To the WARDER:]*
Excuse me, please. I don't mean to interrupt…

    *[FRANKIE and the WARDER are taken
    aback at the intrusion.]*

… but won't you introduce me?

WARDER:    This sorry human being
Is Frankie Fraser.
Sorry, Mr Novello,
He's scum of the earth,
But we're short of cells,
Couldn't find you anything better.
We'll move you when we can.

IVOR:    You're too kind.

WARDER:    *[To FRANKIE:]*
And you behave yourself

With Mr Novello.
We'll be watching you like hawks.

*[WARDER leaves. FRANKIE stares after him aggressively. IVOR steps cautiously forward.]*

IVOR:          Good afternoon, Mr Fraser.
               I'm Ivor Novello,
               But I'd be grateful
               If you would call me Ivor.

*[He holds out his hand.]*

FRANKIE:       *[Menacing]* Are you queer?

*[IVOR drops his hand.]*

IVOR:          What makes you think that?

FRANKIE:       You're in the theatre.

IVOR:          Is everyone in the theatre queer?

FRANKIE:       You tell me...

IVOR:          Quite a few, it's true.
               I have a show running at the Adelphi
               Called *The Dancing Years;*
               I've heard it called *The Prancing Queers...*

*[FRANKIE laughs, and it breaks the ice.]*

FRANKIE:   The prancing queers! That's a good one!
           *[Suddenly menacing again]* But are you?

IVOR:      What can I say?
           If I say yes, you'll do me over –
           Is that the phrase?
           If I say no, you'll still be wondering.

FRANKIE:   Leave it out.
           I've got to know, ain't I?

IVOR:      Frankie, I am theatrical.

FRANKIE:   I know that.

IVOR:      And, yes, I'm musical.

FRANKIE:   That too.
           But – are you?
           I need to know if I've got to watch my arse.

IVOR:      Frankie, I assure you:
           You'll have no need to watch your arse.
           Quite the contrary…

           I'm Ivor, pure and simple,
           A boy from the valleys
           Who wants everyone to like him.

I decided at a very early age
I would be very nice to everyone,
However difficult it was.
I find it pays –
I get nice friends in return.
Friends?

*[IVOR approaches FRANKIE and offers his hand.]*

It will be much easier for both of us
If we can be friends.

*[FRANKIE takes his hand.]*

What are you here for?

FRANKIE:   It's like I told the warder;
They had me stitching mail bags –
Eight stitches to the inch
You have to do!
Screw said I wasn't doing enough
And belted me –
Belted me while I was sitting down,
A sack in my hands.
I ask you, is that fair?

IVOR:   Doesn't sound fair at all.

FRANKIE:   So they put me on pounding
As a punishment.

You have to break up slates so small
The bits go through a sieve.
Ten and a half hours a day!
And when you done it,
The screws, who watched you all day long
In little sentry boxes,
Chuck the cunts away.
What's the point in that?
And it totally fucks your elbows,
If you'll pardon my French.
I wouldn't do it.

IVOR:          Can't say I blame you.

FRANKIE:       So they sent me here;
               They think I'm not all right in the head –

IVOR:          Will they make me sew mailbags?
               You hear such awful stories…
               Do they still have the treadmill?
               That's how they broke Oscar Wilde,
               On the treadmill in here.

FRANKIE:       Who?

IVOR:          Oscar Wilde. Do they still have it?

FRANKIE:       *[Shakes his head]* Nah.
               Ain't had that for forty years.
               You might not think it, but

It's better than it was.
I know an old lag here –
Johnny Ryan –
He was a boy soldier in India.
Chinned a Sergeant,
Got ten years.
That was sixty years ago.
You couldn't see or talk to other cons
In those days.
On exercise they put you in a hood,
Hand on the shoulder of the man in front
To guide you,
Like a fucking centipede.
Only one to see was right in front,
A trusty.

Johnny was in Stafford nick
With cons who saw men hanged in public…

IVOR:          Do they still pick oakum?
Wilde picked oakum.

*[He quotes:]*
'We tore the tarry rope to shreds
With blunt and bleeding nails…'

Please tell me they don't pick oakum.
I'll do anything but that,
It will ruin my hands.
I'll never play the piano again.

FRANKIE:    Nah, they won't make you do that.
            You're a toff, you are.
            Look at the screws,
            Fighting with themselves
            For the chance of crawling up your arse.

IVOR:       I don't want any special treatment.

FRANKIE:    Sure you do;
            You've had it all your life,
            You're soft as shit.
            They'll have you in the library, no fear,
            And playing in chapel Sunday.

            *[Sneering]* Your friends will bring your own
                clothes,
            And nice little tins of patay dee foy grass,
            And cartons of fags –

*[An awkward pause]*

IVOR:       Do you have a cigarette?

FRANKIE:    I got a bit of snout. *[He produces a tobacco
                pouch.]*
            Not much, mind; go easy on it.

IVOR:       *[Bewildered]* What do you do with it?

FRANKIE:    *[Resigned]* Here. Give it here.

314

*[IVOR hands the pouch back.]*

> You're like a fucking baby, you are.

IVOR:        I'm sorry.

*[FRANKIE starts rolling a cigarette.]*

FRANKIE:      What do you usually smoke?

IVOR:        Abdullas. Turkish Number Five Plain.
                I'm never without one,
                I must smoke sixty a day.
                I wish I had one now.

FRANKIE:      Nice, very nice. Cost a bomb.
                *[He gives IVOR a very thin roll-up.]* Here.

*[IVOR lights it with a match, coughs. FRANKIE laughs.]*

FRANKIE:      You'll get used to it,
                Till your own come.

IVOR:        Thank you.
                I'll share mine with you, of course.

FRANKIE:      Too right you will.

*[Sharing the cigarette, they smoke a moment in companionable silence.]*

FRANKIE: I had Abdullas once,
Lorry-load of cartons
From a warehouse in West Ham.
Lovely smoke.
My first job,
Stole three packets of Players,
Got sent to borstal.
Well I had to, didn't I?
Six of us kids…
Mum had three cleaning jobs…
I stole to bring some extra money in,
Quid here, quid there…

I used to swim in the Thames
In the nude, with the rats,
And catch the coins they threw
From the pleasure boats…
Till I got too old
And me balls dropped…
Only the young 'uns got the sympathy.

IVOR: Superannuated at thirteen, how sad!
What did you do then?

FRANKIE: Took to the ring, didn't I?
Sure beat working,
Smashin' someone's face in.

*[IVOR grimaces.]*

Never made much money,
Did it for the love of it.
Nothing like the feeling
When you see a face
That's a bloody pulp.

IVOR: *[Shudders, distasteful]* How could you?
Aren't you scared you'll lose your looks?

FRANKIE: Ha! What looks?

IVOR: You're a fine looking boy.
You could do well in pictures.

FRANKIE: Really?

IVOR: When this dreadful war is over.

FRANKIE: Dreadful? I love this war.

IVOR: I hate this war.

FRANKIE: I grew up in the blackout in this war.

IVOR: I cried when Neville Chamberlain
Came back from Munich,
Waving his piece of paper.

FRANKIE We'd go and nick a car,

IVOR:          Cried with relief.

FRANKIE:       Smash a window,
               Nick some lengths of cloth
               Or ladies' stockings.

IVOR:          I saw it on the newsreel
               With Noël Coward.
               He got so angry with me at my reaction
               That he hit me.
               But I thought things would carry on
               Exactly as before.

FRANKIE:       Before the war, the big boys
               Went for jewellery and furs;
               There were safes for the safe-crackers.
               Now there's so much money
               And stuff around –
               Cigarettes, sugar, clothes,
               Petrol coupons, clothing coupons,
               Scotch under the arches
               At London Bridge.

IVOR:          Will we get bombs in here?

FRANKIE:       Air raids are the best…

IVOR:          What happens in an air raid?

FRANKIE:       …when they're all down the shelter

And leave their front doors open.
No police around, see –
All been called up.

IVOR:          I don't think I can stand it.
               I don't think I can take the noise,
               My ears are very sensitive.

FRANKIE:       I love this war.
               Headlights blacked out –
               No way to read
               Your number plate.

               Everyone's a thief:
               Steal stuff, sell to a man,
               Man sells to the shops,
               Shops sell to folks like you,
               Sell stuff without the coupons.

IVOR:          Except I got caught,
               And sentenced to twenty-eight days.

FRANKIE:       Everyone is at it,
               And it's wonderful!

IVOR:          I hate the war.
               I should have done my fire watching
               On the roof of the Aldwych,
               But I fled to the shelter.
               I'm not proud I fled to the shelter.

FRANKIE:     They tried to get me in the army,
             But I went AWOL three times.
             They recruit in prisons, see?
             They'll take anyone who'll march
             Into the mouth of a machine gun.

IVOR:        You see? We're both the same!

FRANKIE:     Both the same?

IVOR:        You fled from the army,

FRANKIE:     Fled from the army, sure…

IVOR:        I fled from the bombs.

FRANKIE:     …but not cos I was scared,
             Because I liked my life.

IVOR:        [Delighted] As I liked mine.
             Does nothing scare you?
             I so admire that.
             I wish that I was like that.

[FRANKIE is on the verge of a confession, which is not something that comes easily to him, but IVOR turns the full force of his gaze and his personality on him.]

IVOR:        Yes?

FRANKIE:    It's – what the warder said.
            They're going to fry my brain.

IVOR:       No!

FRANKIE:    They say I'm sick,
            I'm – what's the word? –
            A psychopath,
            Incurable.
            They want to take me
            To Banstead Asylum
            For electric shock treatment.

IVOR:       No! You poor, poor boy!
            You must not let them.
            I had a – friend –
            Who – did something rather stupid.

FRANKIE:    What?

IVOR:       Never mind, it doesn't matter,
            But he was caught,
            And ordered to have – treatment.
            They gave shocks into his genitals,
            They gave shocks into his brain.
            He was tied down to the bed,
            A huge bung in his mouth
            To stop him screaming.
            He told me that the worst part
            Was the smell of his own hair and flesh

Burning...
Finally, when all else failed,
They gave him a lobotomy –
An ice pick in the frontal brain
Through the eye socket.

Now he is a husk,
No memory, no emotion.
A zombie...

FRANKIE:    Blimey!

IVOR:       Promise me you'll never let them
            Do that to you.
            Nothing justifies such treatment.

FRANKIE:    *[Stressed, anxious]* I must get out of here...

IVOR:       I'll speak for you;
            I can help, I have money.

FRANKIE:    I'll go on hunger strike.

IVOR:       I'll find you a solicitor.

FRANKIE:    I'll kill someone.

IVOR:       I can write to the Home Secretary.

FRANKIE:    I'd rather hang than not be me.

*[The door opens and the WARDER enters.]*

WARDER:      Time for lunch.
You come down to the canteen,
Mr Novello.

IVOR:      And my friend Frankie?
Can he come with me?

WARDER:      He's on lockdown,
He's too dangerous.
He stays here,
His food comes on a tray.

IVOR:      Please let him come.
I need a friend for moral support –
I'll vouch for him.

WARDER:      I'm sorry, Mr Novello,
You ask too much.

IVOR:      I don't want to face the world alone.
Look at me –
There's nothing to hide behind.
No make-up, no glamour…
Let me stay with Frankie.

WARDER:      No, Mr Novello,
You must.
The other prisoners expect you;

The warders want to meet you.

*[CLARA reappears at IVOR's side, unseen by the others.]*

CLARA:      Ivor, have no fear.
Trust your personality
And your God-given talents.
No-one ever could begrudge you anything.
When you talk to people,
It makes them feel good.

*[CLARA slowly moves away from IVOR.]*

Remember Ivor, you are beloved of the
    gods.
When you were born you cried in perfect
    thirds.

*[CLARA slowly fades away off-stage.]*

IVOR:      This petty regulation will be the end of me.
I have always been surrounded by people
Who loved me.
When the Justice sent me down,
I thought that on my own I'd 'find myself':
Some rare new sense of wisdom;
Some revelation;
Some depth for my shallow soul.
But no, not at all.
I have learnt nothing,

I am just the same,
But bitter, bruised and angry.
Oh Christ, help get me through this
And come out sane.

*[CLARA reappears – they all gather round IVOR vying for his attention. This is a quartet that interweaves, but is here separated for clarity, as before.]*

IVOR:        One day, in maybe five weeks' time,
             I must walk onstage once more
             As Rudy Kleber;
             Again create the dream.
             But now the fantasy is ever tainted
             With sordid memories –
             I don't think I can ever act again.

CLARA:       They love you, Ivor.
             They have always loved you,
             And they always will.
             You threw your heart
             At the feet of every audience;
             They always picked it up.
             Give them your heart now…

FRANKIE:     For Gawd's sake, Ivor,
             It's just a bite of lunch:
             Some horrible mince
             And some old grey spuds.
             It isn't life or death.

You'll be back in half an hour,
Keep your pecker up.

WARDER: I'm sure you'll find
It's better than you think.
Everyone is so excited
And eager to see you,
Shake your hand.
You have no shortage of admirers here.

*[Offstage the prisoners start singing – the on-stage characters sing over them.]*

CHORUS: Keep the home fires burning,
Though your hearts are yearning;
Though your lads are far away
They dream of home.
There's a silver lining
Through the dark clouds shining.
Turn the dark cloud inside out
Till the boys come home

CLARA/WARDER: You see? They really love/like you, Ivor.
You have won your place in their
hearts,
And nothing can dislodge you now.
Let them give you courage,
Let them give you strength.
You are a star, Ivor,
Always a star.

WARDER:     Can I have your autograph, please?

FRANKIE:    What's that tune? I know that tune...
            I remember that from when I was a kid!

            *[He hums a fragment.]*

            Blimey, did you write that?

*[The off-stage chorus ends.]*

            Just wait till I tell Ruby, Mike and Jock.
            The gang'll not believe it.
            Ivor Novello!
            I shared a cell with Ivor Novello!
            And he was such a gent, a real gent,
            I felt happier just for being with him.
            And Ivor, I'll get out unbroken,
            Just you see –
            Unbroken!

IVOR:       I know no other way to live,
            Except in glamour, music and romance.
            My heart is all I give –

CLARA:      Impervious to fashion –

FRANKIE:    No more fears –

WARDER:     This too will fade to nothing down the years.

IVOR:           I can do nothing else but entertain –

CLARA:          And give the tired world a chance to dream –

IVOR:           My glittering stage impervious to pain.

CLARA/WARDER:   An ageless world where smiles reign
                        supreme –

CLARA/IVOR/WARDER:
                The force of charm, the force of fantasy,
                Admits no doubt, and no reality.

FRANKIE: *[Simultaneous over last line]*
                I'll have no doubt, my course is clear to see.

*[IVOR separates himself from the group and proposes a toast in a battered water mug.]*

IVOR:           To life –

OTHERS:         To life.

IVOR:           To love –

CLARA/WARDEN:   To love.

FRANKIE:        For me

IVOR:           To dance –

328

CLARA/WARDEN:   To dance.

FRANKIE:   Escape

IVOR:   To music –

CLARA/WARDER:   To music.

*[The WARDER leads IVOR out of the cell. CLARA disappears into the darkness.]*

FRANKIE:   To Freedom!

*[The cell door shuts. FRANKIE sits rather sad and alone, as off-stage the prisoners are heard humming part of 'Keep the Home-fires Burning', gradually fading with interjections from:*

IVOR:   – silver lining…
   – dark cloud shining….
   – Turn the dark cloud inside out.

PRISONERS:   Till the boys come home.

A SLOW FADE TO BLACKOUT

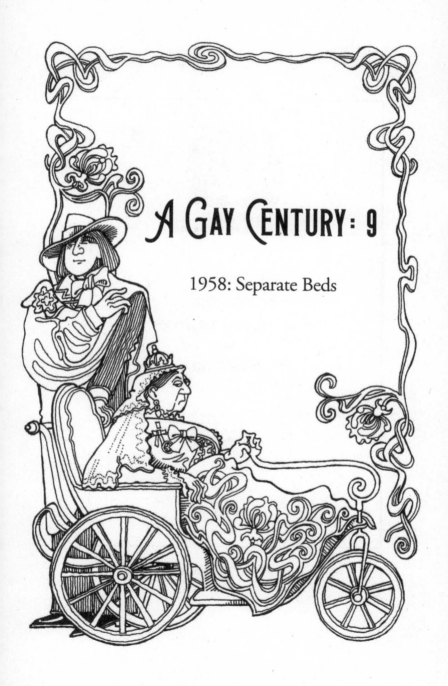

# A Gay Century: 9

## 1958: Separate Beds

**HOME OFFICE**
**SCOTTISH HOME DEPARTMENT**

# Report

## of the Committee on

# Homosexual Offences
## and
# Prostitution

*Presented to Parliament by the Secretary of State for the Home Department
and the Secretary of State for Scotland
by Command of Her Majesty
September 1957*

*LONDON*
**HER MAJESTY'S STATIONERY OFFICE**
FIVE SHILLINGS NET

Cmnd. 247

Above: *Cover of the 1957 Wolfenden Report*

# INTRODUCTION

I owe the idea for two of the operas in this series to old friends. Andrew Lumsden gave me the idea for *'Fishing'* when he told me the story that he'd been told by a friend of how the friend met Lord Alfred Douglas in the 1930s.

Eric Thompson, the partner of Antony Grey, told me this one. In the early 1960s Antony became the secretary of the Homosexual Law Reform Society (HLRS), the campaigning body set up to persuade Parliament to implement the Wolfenden Report and decriminalise sex between men.

They had recently moved into a flat in West Hampstead; their good friend Esmé Langley, the founder of the lesbian magazine *Arena 3* and of the women's Minority Research Group, lived down the road, along with several other homosexuals, singly or in pairs. As a result, among themselves, they called the road 'Queer Street'.

One evening there was a terrific noise in the street. Eric and Antony rushed to the window, to see that a car had wrapped itself round a lamp post. People were already hurrying to help. However, their first thought was – 'Police!' They'd be on the scene to investigate the crash in no time; maybe they'd go house to house to question possible witnesses as to what had happened. If they did, how would they react to two men who not only shared a flat, but also, quite obviously, a bed?

If this seems like over-reactive paranoia, the journal of the HLRS was full of cases in which groups of men had been prosecuted for consensual activity in private – eleven in Lancashire, ten in Swansea – with fines or up to five years in prison in consequence, not forgetting the newspaper publicity. Some of those cases, dredged up by chasing ancient contacts in people's address books, went back over ten years.

For the next ten minutes Eric and Antony raced against time to distribute clothing and bedding between their room and the spare room, to create the illusion that they were 'only' flatmates. They could quite easily have been arrested, maybe even imprisoned, if the police thought otherwise, which would scupper Antony's law reform work and stymie the career of Eric, a high-flying civil servant.

This was the reality of those dark days, deep fear and panic. And yet the spectacle of moving clothes and bedclothes around the flat also had elements of a Whitehall farce.

I decided there would be enough pain and fear in this cycle, and there was a need to lighten the tone occasionally. So, I took the story down the farcical route, with an undertow of that grim reality. I moved Esmé Langley from down the road, into the flat upstairs, and added a couple of plot twists. Antony Grey was a pseudonym. He avoided using his real name, Edgar Wright, in public, to avoid causing his parents embarrassment or pain by association with the cause of homosexual rights. This was a benevolent hypocrisy of which he was conscious.

In all these operas I have imagined a traditional operatic composer as providing the kind of musical 'ambience' of the piece. Often, I have kept that thought to myself, because Robert is very much his own man as a composer, but it has helped me to find the shape of the words. Here we were very much in the comic opera world of Rossini or Donizetti. As a result, the libretto is more intricate and heavily rhymed, and goes like the clappers.

That is why on paper this is one of the longest opera libretti in the cycle; in practice, Robert has more than kept up, and it comes out in performance at just under an hour.

Being the first of the operas which doesn't deal with the Great and the Good, there are no literary sources other than the letter to *The Times* of March 7th, 1958, which kicked off the process of campaigning for homosexual law reform when the Tory government was dragging its feet.

CAST

**EDGAR :** Baritone
*A lawyer, 30-ish, quite conventional. Tall and stooped. Owlish, a little intimidating. For the last five years he has been living with —*

**ERIC :** Tenor
*His partner, slightly younger, a high-flying civil servant making his way up the higher echelons of the Home Office.*

**ESME LANGLEY :** Mezzo
*A large, rather butch lesbian with a penchant for Army Surplus clothing. The upstairs neighbour. She has a rather hearty manner, a cross between Hattie Jacques in Matron mode, and Joyce Grenfell. A great friend.*

**PC ALLCOCK :** Bass
*Young, keen and very good-looking policeman.*

SETTING

ERIC and EDGAR's first floor flat in West Hampstead. The wide hall passage runs directly upstage to the front door at the back, facing the audience. We are to imagine off in the wings on each side are the main bedroom (Stage Right) and the spare bedroom (Stage Left). These two rooms face each other across the passage between front stage and the front door at the rear. The kitchen is offstage Front Right nearest the audience. Near the front door is a plaster model of Michelangelo's David. A chair also in the hall.

INSTRUMENTS

Piano, violin, cello

SEPARATE BEDS

The action is continuous…

*[It is March 7th 1958, early evening. EDGAR is in the hall, dusting The David with a feather duster. A radio offstage in the kitchen is playing Rossini's 'Zitto Zitto Piano Piano' from 'La Cenerentola' on the Third Programme. EDGAR is singing along, conducting with the duster.]*

EDGAR:        'Zitto zitto, piano piano;
                Senza strepito e rumore:
                Delle due qual è l'umore?
                Esattezza e verità.

                'Sotto voce a mezzo tuono;
                In estrema confidenza:
                Sono un misto d'insolenza,
                Di capriccio e vanità'.

*[EDGAR stops dusting and goes into the kitchen during this. As he goes, ERIC lets himself in at the front door and hums along. EDGAR stops singing and turns off the radio.]*

EDGAR:        Is that you, darling?

ERIC:          Well, who did you think it was? The Special Branch?

EDGAR:        They have a key, I'm sure.

*[He reappears in an apron, with a frying pan.]*

And they tap our phone.

ERIC:              But they don't sing along to Rossini.
                   Special Branch is not musical,
                   And they don't ask if you love them.

*[ERIC holds and squeezes EDGAR.]*

Do you love me? Do you?
                   Or has someone else caught your eye?

EDGAR:             Well... There was a rather nice builder
                   In the cottage at the end of the road.

ERIC:              Are you sure he was a builder?

EDGAR:             Cement dust on his boots.
                   I thought he'd suit me fine –
                   But then I thought,
                   More Eric's type than mine.

ERIC:              So generous. Thank you.

*[He turns abruptly as if to go out of the front door.]*

Well, I'll just be off then,
                   And see –

EDGAR:        *[Grabbing him back]*
Oh no you don't –
I'm starving.
I mean for food.
I bought some lamb chops.

ERIC:        Yum. I love tasty little baa lambs.
Whenever I see one in a field,
Suckling its mother,
Shivering its sweet little tail,
I always go 'Aaah',
And think 'Mmm... Leg of lamb'.

EDGAR:        Would you like a drink?
I got a rather fine Amontillado
From the Wig and Pen.
I dropped in for a quick one after court,
Brought a bottle home.
It's an Amontillado del Puerto.

ERIC:        Very nice.
Do you want the paper?

*[He gives EDGAR a copy of 'The Times'.]*

There's a letter urging the government
To implement the Wolfenden Report.
It's signed by loads of people.
Clement Attlee's one of them,
And Bertrand Russell.

EDGAR:     At last. There's been six months' silence
           Since The Report. And over what?
           All that mighty labour for a mouse.

*Duetto: We can't do it*

           We'll be able to have sexual relations,
           But only in specific situations:

ERIC:      If we're either of us under 21 –
           We can't do it;

EDGAR:     If we're staying in a hotel just for fun –
           We can't do it;

ERIC:      If we're living in a flat,

EDGAR:     Or a bedsitter at that,
           Then we have to tell you flat –

BOTH:      We can't do it;

EDGAR:     In Derry 'cross the sea –
           We can't do it;

ERIC:      If we're living in Dundee –
           We can't do it;
           Or in any colony –

BOTH:      We can't do it;

EDGAR:      Guernsey, Jersey,
            Isle of Man –
            We can't do it,

ERIC:       In the Isle of Wight
            We can –
            We can do it.

EDGAR:      Though they're sure to disapprove
            And call us 'queer' and 'poove',
            And we'd really rather move
            So we can do it.

ERIC:       In the army with a soldier –
            We can't do it.

EDGAR:      In the air force with an airman –
            We can't do it.

ERIC:       In the navy with a seaman,
            Though he's ever such a he-man,
            Still the seaman's not a free man –
            We can't do it.

EDGAR:      And even if we are allowed to do it,
            We're still not permitted to meet.

ERIC:       We can't say hello in the street,
            Though we are very discreet.

EDGAR:      We can't importune
            A guard or dragoon;

ERIC:       We might have opportunity,
            But never with impunity;

EDGAR:      So why do we cherish this mouse of a bill
            And Wolfenden hail as a hero?

ERIC:       There's little to give us a cause for a thrill,
            But still it is better than zero.

                        *


*[He gives ERIC the paper back and goes into the kitchen. ERIC
pours two glasses of sherry. Sniffs his. Swills it appreciatively.]*

ERIC:       A fine amontillado indeed –
            Just the relaxation I need:
            Flavour rolling on the palate,
            Vapour strolling round the brain –
            Others may like oloroso,
            But to me it's only so-so;
            Any true aficionado
            Only drinks amontillado –
            Finer than the finest of champagne.

*[He opens the paper, finds the Letters Page.]*

            Where is the Letters Page?

Ah, here it is!
'Sir!' – never 'Dear Sir'.
The editor of *The Times* cannot be a Dear;
*[Spoken]*
'We the undersigned would like to express
Our agreement with the Wolfenden Report.
Homosexual acts committed in private
Between consenting adults
Should no longer be a criminal offence.
The continued enforcement of the present
    law
Will do more harm than good…
Legislation… early date…
Widest support from humane men
Of all parties.'

*[EDGAR comes back during this and takes his sherry.]*

EDGAR:        And what of inhumane men?
There are enough of them
In all parties as well.
So many MPs worry
That if they endorse a bugger's charter,
They will be tainted as Hell.

ERIC:        But it's such a timid little bill –
Over twenty-one, in private,
A mouse of a bill as you said –
Eek! Eek! *[Ad lib.]*

EDGAR: Parliament is full of cats,
Ready to kill your mouse stone dead.

\*

*Duetto: Wolfenden the Mouse*

ERIC: Eek! Eek! Eek!
My name's Wolfenden, don't kill me!
Eeeek!

EDGAR: Poor little Wolfenden!
We don't want to alarm you,
We certainly won't harm you,
You've got to stay alive.

ERIC: Eeek! Eeek! Eeek!

EDGAR: We'll make you grow and thrive.

EDGAR: Wolfenden the mouse,
You're welcome in our house.
We'll make you big and fat,
Almost like a rat.

ERIC: The Tories will be scared of you
After we have cared for you.

EDGAR: The Labour Party too,
Which hasn't got a clue.

ERIC:      We'll both keep you alive,
           We'll make you grow and thrive.

EDGAR:     And what about the Liberals?

ERIC:      Who? Them? There's only five.

EDGAR:     We'll give them all some backbone,
           And we'll tell them what to do,

ERIC:      However much they grouse.
           Don't worry, little Wolfenden,

EDGAR:     Don't worry, little mouse.

BOTH:      You'll always have a welcome in this house.

*

EDGAR:     Dyson is a name that I remember.
           He wrote to *The Spectator* weeks ago
           To start a new campaign.
           What do we know about him?

ERIC:      He's at the University in Bangor.

EDGAR:     He's moved fast. We should join him.

ERIC:      I'll write to him at the university.

EDGAR:        After dinner. *[Realisation]* Aagh! The chops!

*[He rushes to the kitchen. Returns with a smoking frying pan.]*

                       Ah well, charcoal's very good for you,
                       Purifies the blood, they say.

ERIC:          Yum! Burnt bits! My favourite!

*[There is an enormous car crash offstage. ERIC and EDGAR run to the window – by the front door, at the back – and look out.]*

ERIC:          Oh my God! That car's run into a tree!

EDGAR:        It was trying to avoid a cyclist, I think;
                       He's lying in the road.

ERIC:          We must help him. He may be dead.
                       And what about the motorist?
                       What about the tree?

EDGAR:        There are others out there already,
                       We'll only get in the way.

ERIC:          You mean, you don't want to get involved.

EDGAR:        And with very good reason.

ERIC:          We must call an ambulance.

EDGAR:     And that means the police.

ERIC:      Exactly. An ambulance,
           And the police.

EDGAR:     Not the police!

ERIC:      Why not police?

EDGAR:     Not the police, no fear.

ERIC:      The police will have to come.

EDGAR:     That's the last thing we want in here.

*

*Duetto: The police – no police*

ERIC:      There must be the police to investigate the
           crash –

EDGAR:     They'll be coming here and knocking at the
           door.

ERIC:      There's nothing we can do, so don't get in a
           pash.
           They've got to come and ask us what we
           saw.

EDGAR: They'll be coming here inside,
They will have a look round.
And we could go inside
If they act on what they've found.

ERIC: That isn't very likely, so forget this balderdash.

EDGAR: It's very very likely, when they have some
queers to bash.

ERIC: Balderdash!

EDGAR: Queers to bash! *[Repeats x 4]*

ERIC: They'll just want information on that maybe
lethal crash.

EDGAR: If they find some perverts too, they're sure
to make a splash.
See how their figures will be soaring in a
flash!

ERIC: If they've got a crash to deal with, then
they'll be in quite a dash.

EDGAR: We can't take any chances, so we need a
quick precaution.

ERIC: Just calm yourself, it's routine, you should
keep it in proportion.

EDGAR:      We can't have the police –

ERIC:       We must have the police –

EDGAR:      No police…

ERIC:       The police… *[Repeats x 4]*

*[The bell rings.]*

BOTH:       *[In panic]* THE POLICE!

*

*[EDGAR answers the door in trepidation. It is their upstairs neighbour, ESME. She is in her usual fatigues. She is thrilled at the excitement.]*

ESME:       Did you hear that? What a racket!
            That car is a write-off,
            There's glass and metal all over the road.
            Mind you, the Renault Dauphine

            Was always a pile of crud:
            Too much plastic and the brakes of a tortoise.
            Give me a nice nippy Austin Sprite
            For performance;
            Or a Land Army Land Rover,
            Built like a tank
            For endurance.

EDGAR:      Like you, my love, like you.

*[They embrace affectionately.]*

ERIC:      Edgar's in a panic
             About the police.

ESME:      Why, little Eric?
             *[To EDGAR:]* He's in and out of the public facilities
             Like a girl with cystitis,
             And they've never caught him yet.
             Does he think his luck is about to change?

EDGAR:      But they'll come here, Esmé,
             Don't you see?
             They'll look around,
             And they'll find –
             Well, you don't want to know what they'll find.

ESME:      I'm quite unshockable.
             You forget I had two hundred WAAFs
             Under me, and what those girls got up to
             Was nobody's business.
             One up the duff every other day –
             Except the sensible ones
             Of the Radclyffe Hall persuasion.

\*

*Trio: The Girls [Boys] of Summer*

ESME:        Ah! Those girls!
                    The Girls of the summer of '40,
                    Flaxen and brazen and sporty;
                    So lissom and lithe,
                    The smiles so blithe,
                    And more than inclined to be naughty.

                    We'd lie there in the sweet-smelling hay
                    In the heat at the end of the day,
                    And gaze at the cotton-wool clouds
                    In the sky high above;
                    And nobody dared to claim it was love.

                    But it was,
                    Looking back,
                    Yes it was.

                    It was life,
                    It was laughs,
                    It was love.

ERIC:         Ah! Those boys!

EDGAR:         Ah! Those boys!

ERIC:         Those boys on the base at Brize Norton –

EDGAR:         RAF Little Snoring –

ERIC:       So healthy and strong

EDGAR:          All summer long,

ERIC:       And all of them keenly exploring.

ESME:       We'd lie there in the sweet-smelling hay
            In the heat at the end of the day –

EDGAR:      And gaze at the cotton-wool clouds
            In the sky high above,
            And nobody dared to claim it was love.

ERIC:       But it was,
            Looking back,
            Yes it was.

ESME:       But it was,
            Looking back,
            Yes it was.

EDGAR:      But it was,
            Looking back,
            Yes it was.

ALL:        We were in love
            With the girls/ With the boys
            Of summer.

*

EDGAR: *[Coming to]* Have you gone mad?
They'll be here any minute,
And all our things are in there.

*[He indicates bedroom stage right.]*

And there's nothing in the spare bedroom.

*[Indicates left.]*

ESME: Pull yourselves together, boys.
Was this the spirit won the Battle of Britain?
We need a plan,
So act like a man!

ERIC: How can I change the habit of a lifetime?

ESME: Edgar, your things can stay.
Eric, we move your things in here.

*[She indicates stage left.]*

EDGAR: But they're all mixed up.

ESME: No-one's going to look closely to see if the
socks match.

*

*Trio: Quickly quickly*

ESME:      Quickly, quickly, systematic –
           Don't be acting so dramatic.
           Just imagine that you're packing
           For a holiday weekend.

           Quickly, quickly, get them listed –
           You'll forget that they existed
           If you haven't got them written
           Down – on that you can depend.

*[ESME finds pen and paper, writes.]*

ESME:      You'll need underwear, that's vests and pants –

ERIC:      Yes underwear –

EDGAR:     Yes vests and pants –

ESME:      Police will notice at a glance.

*[The trio repeats for as long as it takes to make each transfer from Stage Right to Stage Left, ESME triggering the next one.]*

ESME:      Shoes and socks and shirts and ties –

ERIC:      Shoes and socks –

EDGAR:     And shirts and ties –

ESME:             Police will never realise.

*[They do ties, socks and shirts.]*

ERIC:             Then we have to do the shoes –

EDGAR:            Which is which and whose is whose?

ESME:             Shirts… ties… socks… shoes…

*[They come back with a jumble of shoes.]*

EDGAR:            Those are yours cos you're a seven –

ERIC:             Those are yours, you're an eleven –

ERIC:             Seven…

EDGAR:                Eleven…

ERIC:             Seven…

EDGAR:                Eleven…

ESME:             Oh, for heaven's sake get on –
                  A bobby will be here anon!

ERIC:             Quickly quickly with the trousers –
                  And the jeans too, don't forget 'em!

EDGAR: Quickly quickly with the slacks, if
You forget 'em, you'll regret 'em.

ESME: A jumper and a cardigan,
Pullovers and sweaters.

EDGAR: Playing the charade again
When they come to vet us.

ESME: And what about pyjamas?

ERIC: Well, what about pyjamas?

ESME: You must have some pyjamas –

EDGAR: We never wear pyjamas!

BOTH: Whoever wears pyjamas?

ESME: No pyjamas?

ERIC: No pyjamas.

EDGAR: No pyjamas.

ESME: Some swimming trunks? Or tennis shorts?

EDGAR: We never play those horrid sports.

ESME:          Then finally some blankets,
               Some sheets, a pair of pillows.

ERIC:          Sheets, a pair of pillows –

EDGAR:         Sheets, a pair of pillows!

*[As they bring these out, ESME ticks off her list triumphantly.]*

ESME:          That's everything accounted for,
               There's no more to be said.
               And if they have suspicions still,
               You're sure to kill them dead.

ERIC:          There's just one little problem –

*[He gestures Stage Left.]*

               THERE ISN'T ANY BED!

                              *

*[Aghast. Pause. In the silence, the front door bell rings again.
EDGAR goes to answer it, putting down the sheets in his hand.
ERIC goes to the Stage Right bedroom. At the door, an attractive
young Constable – PC ALLCOCK.]*

ALLCOCK:       May I come in, sir?

EDGAR:         No! – Er – I mean, I don't know…

ALLCOCK:     It's about the accident —
             You might have heard it in the street.
             We're going door to door,
             Asking people to be witnesses.
             We'd like to know if you saw anything,
             Any of you.

*[He is trying to place the three of them. He has casually walked in. He clocks the David.]*

             A fine figure of a lad!

EDGAR:       Who is?

ALLCOCK:     The boy there. *[Pointed]* Big for his age.

EDGAR:       I suppose —

ESME:        *[Taking charge]*
             Good afternoon, constable.
             I am Esmé Langley,
             I work for the BBC Monitoring Unit
             At Caversham.
             And this is my fiancé, Edgar.

EDGAR:       *[Staggering]* Fiancé? Am I?
             Yes, yes, I am.

ESME:        We're getting married next month.
             A quiet wedding, you understand.

> Nothing ostentatious,
> Just the Director General and a few other
>     friends.

*[ERIC re-enters, with some magazines.]*

ESME:       And this is our neighbour, Eric.

ALLCOCK:    *[Attracted] Very* pleased to meet you, sir.

ESME:       He lives upstairs.

ERIC:       Do I?

*[In shock, he drops the magazines. Some physique magazines fall out. ESME gathers them up.]*

ESME:       I buy them for the gardening tips.

*[ERIC and EDGAR instinctively cling together for protection, then realise what they are doing and spring apart.]*

ALLCOCK:    *[Reads]* 'Physique Pictorial'…

ESME:       The exercises are so bracing.

ALLCOCK:    Incorporating 'Adonis' and 'Body Beautiful'.

ESME:       I'm sure we all appreciate a body beautiful.

ALLCOCK:      *[Eyeing ERIC]*
              I'm sure we all do –
              In an artistic way.

ESME:         I'm forgetting my manners, Constable –
              Can you have a name when you're on duty?

ALLCOCK:      Allcock –

ESME:         I beg your pardon?

*[ERIC perks up.]*

ALLCOCK:      Constable Allcock.

ERIC:         *[Murmurs]* Allcock by name…

ESME:         Would you like a cup of tea, Constable
                 Allcock?
              While I make it, why don't you ask some
                 questions
              Of my fiancé and our friend?

*[Horrified, ESME notices among the bedsheets which had been dropped by EDGAR a large dildo.]*

              And if you'll excuse me,
              I must get on with the supper.
              A woman's work is never done!

ALLCOCK:     That's very kind of you, madam.

ESME:        Esmé, please.

*[She covers the dildo in a sheet and exits. EDGAR sits.]*

ALLCOCK:     Did you see anything, Mister –

EDGAR:       Wright.

ALLCOCK:     Mr Wright, are you? *[Pointedly, to ERIC:]*
             And is he? Mr Right?

ERIC:        He is. But I prefer to call him Edgar.

EDGAR:       We're just chums, Constable.

*[They slap backs heartily in an unconvincing attempt to be chums.]*

ALLCOCK:     Lived here long, have you?

EDGAR:       Five years. I don't mean *here*, not in this flat.

ERIC:        What do you think we are?

EDGAR:       In this block. Together in this block.

ALLCOCK:     It must be nice to have an obliging neigh-
             bour –

If you run out of sugar.
Or if you need a *fag* –

EDGAR:     Indeed!

ALLCOCK:   Do you often need a *fag*?

EDGAR:     I prefer to roll my own.

ALLCOCK:   I find I'm always running out.
           Always on the *bum*...
           For a *fag*...

*[Re-enter ESME, with tea.]*

ESME:      I assumed you liked it strong. *[She exits.]*

ALLCOCK:   Yes, thank you. I like it very strong.
           Hot, strong and sweet, that's me.

*Aria/Duet/Trio: Hot Strong and Sweet*

ALLCOCK:   Hot strong and sweet,
           That's something you can't beat.
           When you want to rest your feet,
           Make your happiness complete
           By taking something hot,
           Something strong,
           Something sweet.

ERIC:        I like something hot too –

ALLCOCK:     It's something that you've got to –

ERIC:        Something hot –

ALLCOCK:        Something strong –

ERIC:        And I felt it all along.

ALLCOCK:     Nothing wrong with wanting something
             strong.

ERIC:        And something sweet –

ALLCOCK:        Yes something sweet –

EDGAR:       But quite discreet –

ERIC:           Oh yes, discreet –

ALLCOCK:     Nothing like some hot sweet tea –

ERIC:        That's the ideal tea for me.

ALLCOCK:     Me too.

EDGAR:          Get you!

*

*[Re-enter ESME. She has a bowl (mortar) with some spices in it. She casually returns to the sheets, and nonchalantly picks up the large dildo and starts using it as a pestle. She is 'hiding it in plain sight'. She grinds spices vigorously.]*

ESME:          There's nothing like the flavour of freshly
                    ground spices.

*[ESME can see that ALLCOCK and ERIC are attracted. She directs the aria to ALLCOCK.]*

*Aria: Pound and grind*

ESME:          The mustard seed is small and round,
                    The fennel and the cumin too;
                    And every peppercorn is ground
                    To go into a tasty stew.

                    You've got to grind, grind, grind –
                    The flavours all combined;
                    Pound, pound, pound
                    The spices in a mound

                    Press them hard, grind them down,
                    The nutmeg and the mace.
                    Turn the yellow, mix the brown,
                    Crush them to a sticky paste.

                    Grind, grind, grind,
                    The sweet peppers and the hot –

ERIC:          The sweet –

ALLCOCK:          And the hot –

ERIC:          I like it sweet.

ALLCOCK:          I like it hot.

EDGAR:          She'll give it everything she's got.

ERIC/ALLCOCK:          We'll give it everything we've got.

ESME:          I'll give it everything I've got.
          You have to push –

ERIC:          Push –

ESME:          Hard –

ALLCOCK:          Hard –

EDGAR:          So hard –

ESME:          Press and twist –
          It's the action of the wrist.

ERIC:          How can I resist when you insist?
          I will take it like a shot.

ALLCOCK:          That hot sweet tea that fills the mouth,

That swirls around the epiglottis –

ERIC: What a joy! It's on my tonsils.

ALLCOCK: Tell me what is, tell me what is!

*[ERIC and ALLCOCK now only have eyes for each other, and are oblivious to anything else going on. EDGAR sees this, sighs, and picks up the copy of 'Physique Pictorial'.]*

ESME: There's some mace inside my mortar,
And some poppy on my pestle.

ERIC: We can have ourselves a snorter
If we find a way to wrestle.

ALLCOCK: Would you like to see my truncheon?
I assure you, it's gigantic.

ERIC: That would give me lots to munch on
If my hunger drives me frantic.

EDGAR: And I will not be mean
If Eric's getting keen.
No harm done
To let him have his fun.

ALLCOCK: Better a demanding test
Than making an arrest;
If I did that, truth to tell,

I'd have to nab myself as well.

ESME: *[To ERIC:]* Why don't you take him to the flat
That's on the floor above?

ERIC: Sure you won't object to that?

ESME: It's best for making love.
And how could I object to that
When we've established it's YOUR flat?

ERIC: As a solution, it's a dandy;
Not much room here when you're randy.

ESME: *[Aside to ERIC]* I'm glad the flat can come in handy —
Use it any time you like,
Just don't disturb my motor bike.

ALLCOCK: Your motor bike?

EDGAR: *My* motor bike —

*[It is hard to imagine anyone less like a biker than EDGAR.]*

ERIC: *Your* motor bike?

EDGAR: My motor bike:
To strip it down is what I like;

And Eric has the space to spare
To spread the engine here and there,
And leave some parts upon the stair.
If he's got room it's only fair
To let my bike –

ESME:              *[To audience:] My* bike –

ERIC:                  *His* bike –

ESME:          To let the bike be quartered there,
              Where it is easy to repair.

EDGAR:         So easy to repair,
              The bike *I* keep up there.

ESME:          *[To ALLCOCK:]* Would you like to see
              The leather jackets that we wear?

*[ALLCOCK coughs. Aside:]*

ALLCOCK:       If you're in the police
              You don't often find a friend.
              They must frequent the station,
              But all of them pretend.
              I'm longing for some contact,
              If only for a night.
              I'm longing to say 'Yes!'
              And not repress this appetite,

If only for a night.

ERIC: *[To EDGAR:]* It's only for a night –
Do you think I might?

EDGAR: By me that's quite alright.
We promised that we'd always be
Prepared to grant the liberty,
So that the other could be free.
On this we thoroughly agree.

ESME: *[Pointed, to ERIC and ALLCOCK:]*
So you can go, the two of you;
The window in Apartment Two
Has such a panoramic view
Of all the street, that you can see
Just how the car could hit the tree.

*[ERIC and ALLCOCK are in a dream.]*

ERIC: What car?

ALLCOCK: What tree?

ESME: The car that hit the tree
That caused the accident
You came here to investigate,
And now you must corroborate.

EDGAR: That car! That tree!

370

ERIC:            Now if you'll only follow me…

*Finale*

ERIC:            I promise you, you won't be cheated.
                 Once your thorough probe's completed,
                 You'll be satisfied, I'm sure,
                 With things you never saw before.

EDGAR:           You'll be satisfied, we're sure,
                 With things you've never seen before.

ALLCOCK:         Ah! What pleasure is in store,
                 With things I've never seen before!

ERIC:            Quickly, quickly, up the stairwell –

ALLCOCK:         Quickly, quickly, up the stairwell –

ESME:            Don't delay now, say now farewell –

EDGAR:           An astounding revelation
                 Will appear before your eyes.

ERIC:            No regretting the decision
                 After you have seen the vision,
                 The stupendous elevation
                 That within the bedroom lies.

EDGAR:           *[Picking up one of the physique mags:]*

There's splendid consolation
In the pictures in my mags.
They're delightfully immoral,
And they never pick a quarrel,
Be it anal, be it oral,
The most fanciable of fags.

ERIC:        Quickly, quickly, I'm on heat here –

ALLCOCK:     Quickly, sweep me off my feet here –

ESME:        I am filled with satisfaction
             At my altruistic action.

EDGAR:       I have shown him my devotion
             By indulging his emotion.

ALLCOCK:     Though I love police detection
             I prefer a good erection.

ESME:        Though there's only one objection –
             It's not leading to promotion.

ALLCOCK:     I don't care!

ALL:             We don't care!

ESME:        When the fire of passion spreads –

EDGAR:       It lifts our hearts and turns our heads –

ERIC:         And leaves morality in shreds –

ALL:          And sends us all to different/separate beds.

*[ERIC and ALLCOCK exit, waving goodbye to ESME and EDGAR, who collapses on the chair with his magazine. ESME throws up the mortar and pestle in triumph, scattering powder everywhere.]*

BLACKOUT

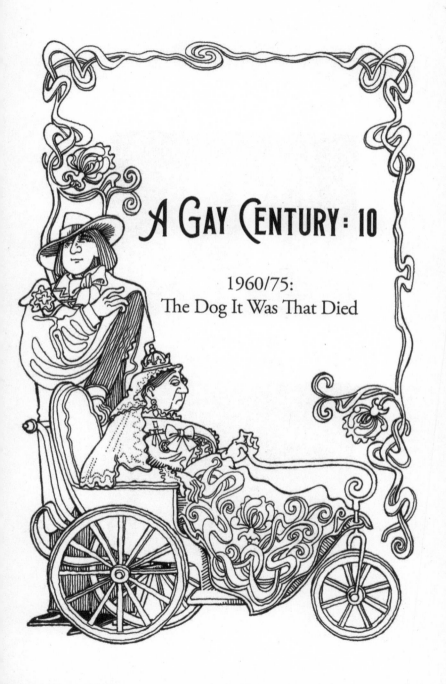

# A GAY CENTURY: 10

### 1960/75:
### The Dog It Was That Died

Above: *Jack Russell*
Below: *Great Dane*

# INTRODUCTION

In May 2018 we were all glued to the three-part BBC-TV series by Russell T. Davies, *A Very English Scandal.* This told the story of Jeremy Thorpe's then-illegal relationship with male model Norman Scott; Scott's obsessive pursuit of the Liberal Leader; Thorpe's botched plot to kill Scott; and the subsequent trial for conspiracy to murder. Hugh Grant was a revelation as Thorpe, Ben Wishaw touching and infuriating as the needy Scott, and the whole story was a classic English comedy of manners of a pitch-black kind.

Watching it, however, I was struck by the role that dogs played in the story. The Great Dane Rinka, the well-known protagonist, unwittingly foiled the murder plot simply by being a dog and getting out of a car at the wrong moment for Walkies. But there was also the Jack Russell, Mrs Tish, who was with Scott when he first had sex with Thorpe at Thorpe's mother's house. Jack Russells are notoriously febrile and energetic. How, I wondered, would an excitable Jack Russell bitch have reacted to the spectacle of two men having sex in the same room as her?

I read the book on which the series was based, by John Preston, which contained even more delectably bizarre details of the case, and discovered that Mrs Tish too died; put down for going on a killing spree in Scott's doctor's hen-coop. Again, she was just being a dog, and paid the ultimate price for it.

Scott was utterly unlucky with people, who treated him rotten. His primary relationships were with animals, especially dogs and horses. Only with them did he find the security and the unconditional affection he craved.

It seemed like the basis of a love story.

*The Dog It Was That Died* revisits these events of the 1960s and 1970s – Thorpe met Scott in 1961 and the chickens came home to roost in 1976 – but sees them entirely through the eyes of the dogs involved. Norman Scott is a mainly off-stage character too, the object of devotion, appearing onstage only in the apotheosis at the end. Thorpe and all the minor characters are non-singing disembodied voices, coming from far away. They may be recorded if necessary, to keep within our discipline of seven performers in total.

This allows for a Liebestod at the end, where Scott, Rinka and Mrs Tish can rhapsodise about the eternal bond between man and dog, who will surely be reunited in Pet Heaven.

Sources:  *A Very English Scandal* by John Preston [Viking 2016]
*Rinkagate: The Rise and Fall of Jeremy Thorpe* by Simon Freeman and Barrie Penrose [Bloomsbury 1997]
*Jeremy Thorpe* by Michael Bloch [Little, Brown 2015]

CAST

**MRS TISH** : Soprano
*A Jack Russell Terrier, quite young. Nervous and highly strung – a little ball of compressed energy.*

**RINKA** : Contralto
*A Great Dane. Immense calm and dignity except where the prospect of a walk is concerned.*

**NORMAN SCOTT** : Tenor
*A man in his 20s – 30s with a history of nervous disorders.*

**PETER BESSELL (spoken), DOCTOR (spoken), ANDREW NEWTON (spoken)** : Played by the same person. May be recorded.

**JEREMY THORPE and DAVID HOLMES (spoken).** May be recorded.

SETTING

The opera has several scenes in different settings, so nothing specific is needed. A low rostrum about 6ft x 3ft distinguishes the human level above the dog level. On it a bed and (later) a car seat.

INSTRUMENTS

Alto, tenor and baritone saxophones, harp

# STYLE

It is important that the events should all be seen from the dogs' point of view, and that the humans should seem strange and alien, except for Scott. This is in part achieved by the way in which the dogs only communicate directly with the audience, and the humans only communicate with each other (except Norman). Where events such as the sex are described in the opera, the actions should not be physically reduplicated. Whether the humans are on or offstage is a matter for the director. I prefer offstage.

Mrs Tish and Rinka should not be dog impersonations – definitely not down on all fours – but should retain dog characteristics.

The parts of the script in **Gill Sans MT** are for events which occur offstage, which the dogs and/or the audience can hear, but not see.

# THE DOG IT WAS THAT DIED

## PART ONE: 1961–62

Prelude:

*[An instrumental prelude, over which, spoken offstage:]*

SCOTT:        Detective Inspector Huntley? I have come to
              tell you about my homosexual relations
              with Jeremy Thorpe, MP.

## SCENE ONE

*[November 1961. A bedroom at the house of Ursula Thorpe, Jeremy's mother. MRS. TISH enters. She sniffs and goes round the edge of the room.]*

MRS TISH:     Mould. Nasty. No-one here long time.
              No heating. Me gonna be cold. *[She sniffs
                  again.]*
              Mouse smell. Definitely mouse smell.
              They got mouses, lots of mouses.
              Maybe me catch. Maybe me eat.
              Nyum, nyum, nyum, nyum.

              Me hungry. No dog food here.
              All me have is boiled egg, like humans.
              Crunch shell, nice, ach, ach, ach, ach,
              But egg boring and make farts.

Me need meat.

My Norma-dog – he pack leader –
He me pack of two – has no dog food.

Poor Norma-dog, has no money.
Poor Norma-dog, has no dog food,
Has no money, poor Norma-dog.
So he go Jemmy-dog,
Who live in big, big stone kennel,
Big clock too – bong! – bong! – bong! –
    bong!
*[The Big Ben prelude to striking the hour]*
Man on horse with sword outside,
But no horse poo, no horse smell,
He no move.

Other humans, real humans, walk down
    corridors.
Me want run after them,
But my Norma-dog tell me no,
We have see Jemmy dog.

*[Mrs TISH sniffs round THORPE's feet in memory.]*

Me like Jemmy-dog, he talk me nice,
Smile me, rub my nose.
He smell nice flowers out of bottle.

And he make me royal! Yes!

Big man say me no can go in big kennel,
But Jemmy-dog says
King Charspannel can go in,
Cos King Chars say so, and me
Might be bit King Charspannel.
So me royal!
And go in, very grand!
Heh-heh-heh-heh. *[She pants.]*

We come in country in Jemmy-dog car.
Jemmy-dog car called Rover!
Me had Cotswold friend called Rover,
We chase round and round.
So now we in country.
Me like country.
Me like smell, simpler smell, sweeter smell.
Petrol? Pah! Pah! Pah!

*[She rubs her muzzle with her paw to get rid of the smell.]*

We stay Jemmy-dog's motherbitch.
She Urse. Yes, you right...
She not Urse-dog, just Urse.
She don't like dogs.
Only humans like dogs are dogs, part of
    pack.

*[NORMAN comes in. MRS TISH leaps to greet him.]*

NORMAN: Hello, Mrs Tish. Who's a good doggie, then?

## Who loves Mrs Tish?

MRS TISH: You do! You do!
Norma-dog loves Mrs Tish,
And Mrs Tish loves Norma-dog.

*[She licks his hand excessively.]*

NORMAN: Now calm down. We've got to sleep. People
want us to be quiet.

MRS TISH: *[To audience:]* He just clean his teeth.
Smell toothpaste.
Nyum, nyum, nyum.

NORMAN: So there's a nice blanket for you to sleep on,
so you won't get cold. Get on the blanket
there.

*[MRS TISH tries to follow him; she wants to sleep on the bed.]*

NORMAN: No. Not here. You can't sleep on the bed, you
leave hairs.

MRS. TISH: *[To audience:]* Me?! Hairs?!

NORMAN: *[Orders]* Blanket!

*[MRS TISH goes and lies down.]*

Good girl, good girl.

MRS TISH:   He got his pills now calm him down.
　　　　　　He take them water.
　　　　　　He sleep now.

NORMAN:   **Night-night, Mrs Tish.**

MRS. TISH:   Night-night, Norma-dog.

*[A huge dog yawn. Puts her head on her paws.]*

**[A click and a creak of the door opening. JEREMY THORPE is coming in.]**

MRS TISH:   Hello? Hello?
　　　　　　What Jemmy-dog doing here?
　　　　　　He has own basket down corridor.
　　　　　　He got jar *[sniff]* smell sweet and sticky.
　　　　　　I think Vaseline.
　　　　　　Norma-dog give Vaseline to me
　　　　　　When I was puppy,
　　　　　　When cat – Grr – scratch my nose.
　　　　　　But me lick it off,
　　　　　　It so nyum, nyum, nyum, nyum,
　　　　　　Make Norma-dog angry.

**[THORPE has come into the room and is sitting on the bed. This could interweave with MRS TISH's lines.]**

NORMAN:     There's nothing wrong, is there?

THORPE:     Should there be? Don't look so scared. You
            look like a frightened little rabbit. Are you
            my little bunny, mm? *[NORMAN starts to
            cry.]* No, don't do that, please don't. I can't
            stand seeing people cry. Not – not people I
            care for.

*[They kiss.]*

MRS TISH:   Funny, how humans have more than one
                skin.
            They have day skin, night skin,
            Special skin for special things
            Like party or dinner or play cricket.
            Me have just one skin,
            Keep me warm, keep me dry, keep me cool.
            Jemmy-dog have special night skin.
            It shiny gold and rustle – oops – no –
            He *two* night skins,
            Take off shiny gold rustly coat, got jim-jams
                now.
            Top and bottom jim-jams like suit,
            Black suit, creamy buttons.

            Norma-dog only have bottoms.
            Stripey bottoms, heh-heh-heh.
            And little vest show real skin.
            Me like real skin, him soft.

Oops – now no bottoms!

NORMAN: No-one's ever been so kind to me before.

[They kiss again.]

MRS TISH: No-one? No-one???
You forgetting?
What about me?
Me always kind, always love my Norma-dog.
Lick face, lick hands,
Sit on lap, lie on bed –
If you let me, if you let me.
And now – 'no-one's been kind to me'!
That's all thanks me get.

THORPE: You see? That wasn't so bad was it? Now I'm
going to do something, very gently I
promise, and I think you're going to enjoy it.
Now turn over, and get on all fours.

MRS TISH: Look, he doggie now!
Norma-dog is real dog.
And Jemmy-dog real dog behind him.
They two doggies, they go aah-aah-aah.
Me join in, what fun!

[Mrs Tish is very agitated, going to and fro.]

No, maybe not. Jemmy-dog be angry.

*[Norman is stifling cries of pain.]*

THORPE:       No don't cry out. No noise. Mother's in the
              next room, she'll hear you through the wall.

MRS TISH:     He hurt my Norma-dog.
              Jemmy hurt my Norma-dog.
              No, stop it, mustn't hurt my Norma-dog.
              Me love him, stop it, now stop it,
              Or me bite your ankles. Stop it.

THORPE:       *[Hissing]* Down, down, Mrs. Tish. Back in the
              corner, go back. Sh! Sh!

MRS TISH:     *[Slinking back]* What could me do?
              That voice, there's no arguing with it.
              Me know Alpha male when me hear it,
              And this Alpha Alpha plus plus male.
              Nothing to do but watch and wait.
              Don't hurt him, Jemmy, don't hurt my baby.
              Cos, in funny way,
              He my leader and my baby same time.

THORPE:       See? That wasn't so bad, was it? And if you
              come to London we can see each other all
              the time. It's getting late now, I'd better go
              back to my room. Urse wakes up very early,
              and she's got ears like a bat. And don't ever
              mention this to anyone, understand?

*[THORPE exits.]*

MRS TISH:     No, don't go London, please.
              Me go anywhere with you, of course,
              You me leader, me love you.
              But please, not with Jemmy.
              He hurt you. He bad for you.
              And I want to chase rats,
              Nyum, nyum, nyum.

*[MRS TISH comes hesitantly over to the bed, and licks NOR-MAN's hand, which is hanging down.]*

MRS TISH:     Mmmm. Vaseline. Nyum, nyum, nyum.

## BLACKOUT

\*

First Interlude

*[Newspaper headlines and pictures from November 1961 to June 1962. Especially THORPE election canvassing pics.]*

SCOTT:     *(Spoken, offstage)* He's got my National Insur-
                     ance Card, you see. And since I walked out I
                     can't very well go back and ask him for it.
                     You're in a position to get me a new one.
                     Could you do that for me? Could you?

\*

SCOTT:     *(As above)* I'm sorry to be a nuisance, but I
                     really do need that National Insurance
                     Card, and you did promise me. Without my
                     National Insurance Card, I can't sign on to
                     register for work, I can't claim unemploy-
                     ment benefits, I can't get another job. My
                     money has almost run out, and I'm getting
                     desperate.

\*

SCOTT:     *(As above)* I'm not well. I can't model any
                     more, I sweat too much. All this stress, not
                     having a job, not having any money, or any-
                     where to live. I've got to get that Insurance
                     Card back. You were my employer. You were
                     my lover. I can't afford to make up the

arrears, it's hundreds of pounds. Please just pay the stamps and give me the Card. That's the least you owe me.

\*

SCOTT:      *(As above)* Look, Mr Steel, you can help me. I haven't got a vendetta against Mr Thorpe. All I want is my Card back. In fact, I still love him. Despite the way he's treated me. I can prove everything I say. I have the letters...

\*

Scene Two

*[May 1962. MRS TISH centre stage. She has blood all round her mouth, and chicken feathers on her coat.]*

MRS TISH:    Me naughty girl. Me know it.
             Couldn't help it.
             Can dog stop being dog?
             Don't know what come over me.

             Hmm, not true.
             Know just what come over me.
             Blood lust; dog lust.
             All the doggy generations calling
             In the blood running through the veins,
             Down the ages.
             Me was wolf once,
             Though you might not think to look at me.

             Chickens. Nyum, nyum. Chickens food.
             Chickens. Nyum. Chickens stupid.
             You start, can't stop.
             You say, keep for later,
             Cos you never know where next meal come.
             But me know where next meal come,
             From Norma-dog.
             Norma-dog feed me before himself.

             No, the blood bubble in the brain
             And in the nose,

392

And the smell of it drive you mad.
The chicken blood mix with your blood,
And all blood cries for more blood,
More chickens.

Chickens taste scrummy.
Nyum, nyum, nyum, nyum.
*[Licks round her chops]* Blood – scrummy.

Shame it was the doctor's chickens.

We go out together, Norma-dog and me.
It's called a 'lection, cos they 'lect someone,
Which means choose and send them
    London.
Norma-dog give people paper,
How marvellous Jemmy-dog is,
And they must send him London again;
He go all round farms.
Lots Walkies, lots fresh air, lovely.
He work stables too, lovely smell horses,
Lots rats to chase as well.
Make chickens fly around, me laugh so
    much.
Heh-heh-heh-heh-heh.

But Jemmy-dog make Norma-dog sad;
Cos he ask Jemmy-dog for papers,
And Jemmy-dog don't send papers.
We sit in offices long time,

Nothing happen and it very boring,
And Norma-dog have no money.
He going crazy.
He go to doctor for pills;
Lorazepam calm him down,
Tuinal make him sleep,
He take lots, and drink too –
He don't know where he is.

He go see Doctor, live in country,
Nice big garden pee and poo in,
He keep chickens down the bottom.
Norma-dog have long time with doctor,
Tell him all 'bout Jemmy-dog,
Pay no mind to me.
Me go sniff round garden,
Me very hungry, smell chickens at bottom.
Nyum nyum nyum.

And there is space in fence under wire,
And chickens go cluck noise,
And look so fat and stupid,
And they so slow, and before me know
Me dig, dig, scratch under fence
Then me inside and have mouth round
    neck
Of nice fat chicken, and me shake and
    shake
Till neck go 'snap!', and blood down throat,
And it is so exciting, so wonderful,

Marvellous and me happy like in dream,
And red everywhere, me see red,
And me chase, me bite and snap,
And drink blood, like me drunk.

And Norma-dog come running and pull me
  out of coop,
And then me see no chickens, only bodies,
And feathers everywhere.
Norma-dog so angry, he beat me –
He never done that –
With tears in his eyes.

Me dog. Why leave me with chickens?
Asking for trouble.
Why can't I have tuinal same as him?

He argue with doctor, who shout at him.
Doctor don't like dogs, he only a human.
Norma-dog beg, plead,
But doctor say, 'I insist',
And take him needle.

Here come Norma-dog now, with doctor.
He got needle for me.
Me have tuinal, maybe.
Goody, goody.
Me calm now.
Me tired, very tired.

DOCTOR: If you could just hold her, she'll stay still for you.

NORMAN: I can't –

DOCTOR: I can get a magistrate's order, you know. Then she'll be put down among strangers, in an unknown place.

NORMAN: No…. please…

DOCTOR: She trusts you. She won't know what's going on. Phenobarbitol is very quick. She won't feel anything. It's best this way.

MRS TISH: Here come my Norma-dog.
I feel safe in his arms.

NORMAN: I love you Mrs Tish.

MRS TISH: I love you too, Norma-dog.

NORMAN: There, there –

MRS TISH: He stroke me so nice.

*[She stiffens slightly as the needle goes in.]*

DOCTOR: That's it. All over.

NORMAN:     Go to sleep now, go to sleep.

MRS TISH:   Sleep....

[*MRS TISH dies.*]

BLACKOUT. End of Part One.

Second Interlude: Passage of time 1962–75

*[Spoken conversation off:]*

THORPE:        There is no other solution.

BESSELL:       We can't just sit and calmly discuss murder in
               the House of Commons.

THORPE:        There is no other solution. What if Scott sells
               his story? I'll be ruined. He would have to
               be shot, Peter. it's no worse than shooting a
               sick dog.

*[The Daily Mirror front page quoting that line flashes up.]*

BESSELL:       It's a bloody sight worse. Scott may be a shit,
               but he's a human being.

THORPE:        In New York, I believe they drop them in the
               river.

BESSELL:       American rivers are deeper.

THORPE:        I read somewhere in America they disposed
               of a body by covering it in fast-setting con-
               crete.

BESSELL:       If you read about it, they must have dis-
               covered it.

THORPE:     *[Dejected]* Oh. *[Brightens]* I know! A tin mine!
            That's the answer. Take Scott to a pub, get
            him drunk, put him in a car, take him out on
            Bodmin Moor, and kill him.

BESSELL:    How?

THORPE:     It's quite easy to break someone's neck.

HOLMES:     But what if I only choke him? What if he
            comes back alive?

THORPE:     You're right, David. In that case you'll have to
            shoot him. Go through his pockets to
            remove any ID, drag him across the moor
            and tip him –

BESSELL:    He's quite a large man. And there's bound to
            be a trail of blood.

THORPE:     You'll have to mind the shit too. When you
            shoot someone they shit themselves, appar-
            ently. You don't want to smell of –

BESSELL:    It'll have to be poison.

HOLMES:     Won't it look rather odd if he falls off his bar
            stool stone dead?

BESSELL:    Just apologise to the landlord and ask him

where the nearest mine shaft is?

THORPE: It'll have to be a slow working poison. Just do your research, David. Then find the man to do it.

\*

Part Two

[*24th October 1975. The Castle Hotel, Porlock; later on Exmoor.*]

[*The rostrum is a bar seat. RINKA is sitting on it, looking disdainfully at the other people in the bar. The sound of rain outside – which runs through the whole scene, louder when the action moves outside.*]

RINKA:        What a common lot of people!

I expected better from the Castle Hotel, Porlock.

Its name holds far more promise than its clientèle.

Look at them. [*Sniffs.*]

I doubt one of them had a bath all week.

Norman has a drink.

I wish I had a drink.

They never think of dogs in these places.

Norman is nervous. His pills aren't helping.

He is waiting for a man. The man is late.

He has no patience.

I have a lot of patience.

I wish Princess Eleanor was here.

She belongs to Norman's friend, so she's my friend.

I call her 'My Princess'.

Other dogs whisper that we're lesbians,

But do not dare to say it to our faces,
Because we are Great Danes.
Hah! Hah!

NORMAN:     Sh, Rinka! You'll get us thrown out.

*[The sound of the rain.]*

RINKA:      I love rain.
I love to run over the moors
With the wet grass under my paws,
And the rain hitting my nose.
Rain tastes very sweet.
Better than tap water.
Maybe we will go for a walk, Norman and
me.
He has an umbrella.

He's getting up. Walkies? Walkies?

*[RINKA follows him outside. The rain is louder.]*

There is a car with lights on,
Waiting up the road.
Let's see.

*[NORMAN goes to the car. RINKA hangs around, eager.]*

NORMAN:     What sort of time is this? I've been waiting an
hour.

NEWTON:     Is that your brute?

RINKA:      Brute? I am the finest pedigree.
            I do not like this common little man,
            He smells of fear and treachery.

NORMAN:     Sort of. She grew too big for my friends, so
            now she's pretty much mine. Isn't she beau-
            tiful? Who's my beautiful Rinka then?

RINKA:      I am. Me, me, me.

[RINKA circles round NORMAN, trying to get in on the conversation.]

NEWTON:     Well, put her somewhere. I can't stand dogs.

NORMAN:     I'm not going anywhere without her.

RINKA:      We go for a drive? We go on the Moors?

NEWTON:     But she's the size of a bloody donkey.

RINKA:      Philistine.
            I am exactly the right size for a Great Dane.
            You have no appreciation of beauty.

NORMAN:     Rinka is Japanese, it means submissive. She's
            very well trained.

RINKA:      Thank you. And so are you.

NEWTON:     All right. Get in the car. Put her on the back
            seat. She'd better not ruin my upholstery.

RINKA:      Call this upholstery?
            I've seen better fabric on a pub tea towel.
            This car is ten years old at least.
            I can barely turn round.
            A Cortina, I ask you!
            I need a Jaguar at least.

NEWTON:     She's soaking wet.

NORMAN:     She doesn't mind.

NEWTON:     I'm not thinking of her.

RINKA:      No, of course you're not thinking of me.
            That's the sort of common little man you
                are.

*[RINKA settles on the back seat.]*

RINKA:      That's better. Now I'm comfy.

*[The car moves off.]*

RINKA:      I can't see anything out of the window
            In this rain.

NEWTON: Are they aggressive, Great Danes?

NORMAN: Of course not. She's a soppy old thing, aren't you?

RINKA: Soppy? I don't think so.
But I do what I am told.
Anything for a quiet life.

NEWTON: But do they attack sometimes? Pedigrees can be temperamental, it's the inbreeding.

RINKA: Temperamental? The very idea.
I am renowned for my even temper.
Children love me, I carry them on my back.

NEWTON: I mean, if someone was to threaten you, what would she do?

RINKA: Threaten Norman?
Who's threatening Norman?
They better not.
I do not trust this man at all.

NEWTON: There's the man from Canada after you.

RINKA: What man from Canada?

NEWTON: Trying to murder you.

RINKA:    This is preposterous.
          How can you believe this tosh?

NEWTON:   And you were beaten up by those thugs. Was
          Rinka with you then?

RINKA:    No I wasn't. But I saw him after,
          And licked his poor bruised face,
          Over and over.

NEWTON:   I'm tired. I'm worn out. I've been on the go all
          day. This rain is killing me.

NORMAN:   Let me drive then.

RINKA:    Norman, you can't drive.

NORMAN:   I've driven tractors.

NEWTON:   I'll stop here.

NORMAN:   I'll get out. You slide over this side. No, don't
          get out, you'll be soaked.

*[NORMAN gets out of the passenger seat, NEWTON gets out of
the car too, RINKA follows him so they are all outside.]*

RINKA:    What a relief to stretch my legs!
          That miserable little car is agony.

Smell the gorse – a smell like coconut.
  *[Sniffs.]*
The heather's past its best.

NORMAN: Oh God, now she'll want to go for a walk.
  Come here, Rinka.

RINKA: No, Norman, come with me.
You'll love it really.

NORMAN: Who's a silly thing? Who's a silly thing?

RINKA: Don't be so childish.
I am not a silly thing,
I have a perfectly reasonable desire
To stretch my legs.
I need a lot of exercise.
I hate it when you talk like that,
So patronising.

NORMAN: Come on girl, come on. Mwa, mwa. Get back
  in the car, we'll all get soaked.

*[NORMAN is trying to get RINKA back in the car.]*

NORMAN: Rinka, come on. Yes, my darling.

*[There is a click of a gun. RINKA hears it, cocks her ear. Looks at NEWTON.]*

RINKA:    It's you.
          You're the man from Canada.

[RINKA turns and runs away. There is a shot. RINKA falls.]

NORMAN:   You've shot my dog.

NEWTON:   Yes, and you're next.

[Click, gun won't fire. Click. Click.]

NEWTON:   Shit, shit! Why doesn't anything ever fucking
          work? Why does everything go wrong?
          Always.

[A car door slams. The car drives off, the sound fades into the
distance. NORMAN walks into the light, onstage, takes RINKA
and cradles her in his arms. He comes forward.]

Epilogue

NORMAN:   I always knew it was wrong,
          But Jeremy infected me
          With homosexuality,
          And now I pay the price.
          No, not me, the dogs.
          I have been the sinner,
          But they have paid the price.

All the human lust and greed
All the selfishness and need-
iness, stampede
For pleasure and for gain,
For power and fame,
And never mind the ones who bleed.

I have never met a man I liked,
Not really.
Men exploit you and they use you,
Let you down, abuse you,
Promise you the earth,
Take everything you're worth.
Tell you lies, give you pain,
Make a vow, then lie again.

Men are lower than the beasts.

And if you fall for them,
Then you become a beast as well.

*[MRS TISH enters, so there is now a ghostly dog backing chorus.]*

All the love I've ever known
Is dogs;
Horses and dogs.
Dogs give love without condition.

MRS. TISH:  We loved you so,
You were our world.

NORMAN:     Horses bear you with devotion,
            Ask for nothing:
            A soft word, a calming hand,
            A bag of oats, a little water,
            And some kindness.

            Will there be dogs in Heaven?
            Do animals have souls?
            If there are no dogs in Heaven
            I don't want to go.

*[RINKA rises and stands the other side of NORMAN from MRS. TISH.]*

TISH:       We have love –

RINKA:          We have trust –

TISH:       Is that not enough?

BOTH:       We will be with you
            Through all your life.

NORMAN:     No more people,
            No more men.
            I will be strong enough
            To be alone,
            With my horses,
            With my dogs,
            With my seventy hens,

> A parrot, a canary
> And a cat.

TISH/RINKA:    No, no cats.

NORMAN:    Yes, a cat,
> Cos animals are good
> As men are bad.

> I have been treated as an animal
> And cast aside,
> While all I love have died.

TISH/RINKA:    We died for you.

NORMAN:    No more the itch of the body.
> I would rather have your love…

TISH/RINKA:    Love –

NORMAN:    …than any touch of man.
> The animals will teach us,
> The dogs will be our guiding star.
> We can be like animals,
> We can be better than we are.

### BLACKOUT

### THE END

# Acknowledgements

At this writing, *A Gay Century* has been in the making for over four years. It has taken a great deal of support to bring it to this stage. First and foremost I must thank Robert Ely, who has now written the music to complete 12 out of the 17 operas. I owe him many inspiring and fruitful discussions on What'sApp, and, between lockdowns, tea and cakes in Fulham. Not forgetting the constant attentions of his dog, Tiger.

While I was researching some of the pieces, the staff at both the British Library and the Bishopsgate Institute were endlessly patient and helpful, and often pointed me to towards sources I would not otherwise have known. There's also a particular thrill in handling a fragile first edition in the BL Rare Books room in gloves.

I have further refined the pieces in the course of presenting them as Zoom readings during two series of lockdown performances by Homo Promos in 2020, and all the actors involved deserve my gratitude:

Mark Bunyan, Fi Craig, Matthew Hodson, Steve Mackay, Alex Hunt, Dan de la Motte, Rich Watkins, Lucie Spence, Catherine Lord, Terry McGrath, John Dawson, Rex Melville, John Anstiss, Patrick Kealey, Ian Lucas, Finlay Jones, Keith Bursnall and Nicola Quinn.

Chris Reilly was an excellent proof-reader; Andrew Lumsden an encourager supreme; Clare Truscott a brilliant Zoom controller; and my partner was never far from my thoughts.

At The Conrad Press I have had a wise and friendly guide through the process of getting the book to market – thank you, James Essinger. And finally I owe a debt of gratitude to my cover designer, the great cartoonist David Shenton [check him out on Facebook], and designer/typesetters Rachael and Nat Ravenlock.

It has been a fruitful and enjoyable experience. We'll meet again – I know where – I know when: On Volume Two, in 2022. Cheers!

*PS-P*

*20th April 2021*

# IMAGE ATTRIBUTION

p. 12, Oscar Wilde on his deathbed 1900, File:Oscar Wilde on his Deathbed 1900 by Maurice Gilbert.jpg - Wikimedia Commons

p. 12, Queen Victoria, 1900. Portrait by Bertha Müller. National Portrait Gallery. http://www.artuk.org/artworks/queen-victoria-157318

p. 40, Sir Arthur Vicars, KCVO: Ulster King of Arms 1900, Library of Congress Prints and Photographs. Bain News Service Collection http://hdl.loc.gov/loc.pnp/ggbain.00685

p. 40, Francis R. [Frank] Shackleton 1900 from the Dublin Herald. http://homepage.eircom.net/~seanjmurphy/images/jewels08.html

p. 40, Irish Crown Jewels, stolen June 1907 – Dublin Metropolitan Police. File:Irish Crown Jewels.jpg - Wikimedia Commons

p. 84, Edward Carpenter [left] and George Merrill c. 1900. Unknown author. File:Carpenter et Merrill.jpg - Wikimedia Commons

p. 84, EM Forster portrait by Roger Fry 1911. File:Portrait of E.M. Forster by Roger Fry, 1911s..jpg - Wikimedia Commons

p. 112, Siegfried Sassoon by Charles Beresford 1917. File:Siegfried Sassoon by George Charles Beresford (1915).jpg - Wikimedia Commons

p. 112, Noël Coward in his teens. File:Noel Coward in his teens.jpg - Wikimedia Commons

p. 112, Robert Ross 1911. File:Robert Ross (1869-1918) nel 1911 in una foto di Elliott and Fry.JPG - Wikimedia Commons

p. 150, Compton Mackenzie c 1924. http://homopromos.org/1928_sauce-gander.html#

p. 150, Radclyffe Hall and dachshund at Crufts, 1923 [cropped from original]. Author Radclyffe Hall, left, and Lady Una Troubridge with their dachshunds at Crufts dog show, February 1923 - Radclyffe Hall - Wikipedia

p. 150, William Joynson-Hicks, 1923, when Minister of Health. File:1st Viscount Brentford 1923.jpg - Wikimedia Commons

p. 202, Eldorado Club 1932 "Here it's Okay!". File:Bundesarchiv Bild 183-1983-0121-500, Berlin, Bar "Eldorado".jpg - Wikimedia Commons

p. 262, Lord Alfred Douglas, by Howard Coster, 1940s. NPG collection. NPG x11380; Lord Alfred Bruce Douglas – Portrait – National Portrait Gallery

p. 296, Ivor Novello, 1949. https://www.bbc.co.uk/staticarchive/e858caea0d0c7e3146cac8afc7263d2caa1cb7f6.jpg

p. 296, Frankie Fraser, late 1940s https://static.wikia.nocookie.net/thekraytwins/images/1/18/Frankfraser.jpg/revision/latest?cb=20170830183050

p. 332, Cover of the 1957 Wolfenden Report. File:Wolfenden Report (31909047460).jpg - Wikimedia CommonsFile:Wolfenden Report

p. 376, Jack Russell Terrier [Mrs Tish double] by Radoslaw Drozdrewski. File:Jack Russell Terrier Demi.jpg - Wikimedia Commons

p. 376, Great Dane, [Rinka double] by Lilly M. File:Dog niemiecki czarny głowa LM980.jpg - Wikimedia Commons